MW01119992

Once Upon a Time:
Fairy Tale Puzzle Quilts

Machine appliqué and embellishment
projects designed to ignite your creativity
and delight your favorite princesses.

By Beth Helfter

Dedications

To Paige, Eva, and Greta
You will always be my princesses.
(And I will always be the Queen.)

And to my Mom,
Who I know is smiling down on her own princess.

Acknowledgements

At great risk of sounding like an Oscar speech, I really must thank so many people without whom this book never would have been possible.

To my husband Joe, who when I threw out the premise behind this book to him while we were driving in the car with three loud obnoxious children in the backseat managed not only to hear me, but to say "I think this is the best idea you have ever had," and mean it. And for the next 5 months shouldered much more of the household and child care burdens than usual, normally with a smile or at the very least without a visible grimace. I love you and could not have done this without your rock solid support.

To my entire family, for eating way too much cold chicken, macaroni and cheese, and Chinese food while I was working on this project. I owe you steak tornados and salmon Florentine ASAP.

To my Dad and Carole, who have been unfailing supporters of EPQD from the very beginning, and enjoy venturing into quilt shops on their travels around North America to talk me up to the owners.

To my sister Alison Miller, whose editorial voice I kept hearing in my head as I wrote, and even now am thinking I need to call and find out if "whose" or "who's" is the proper spelling in this sentence.

To Nancy Dill and the staff of Quiltwoman, for believing in my book concept, and bringing this book to life.

To my many friends who countless times told me "You need to write a book." I know this isn't the kind you meant, but it's a book and it counts. And you were all correct, because now I can't wait to do another.

To the members of Squanicook Colonial Quilt Guild. I still have no idea what our club name means, but I've never met a nicer group of quilters anywhere. And special thanks to Jan Dillon, who taught the continuous binding method on page 79 to me at a Technique Night many years ago and changed my quilting life forever.

And finally to the amazing set of quilters who enthusiastically jumped at the chance to make samples and try things out to be sure they worked: Barbara Chojnacki, Deb Donovan, Linda Leathersich, Jeanne Lex, Renae Mathe, Joany Orsi, Kathy Schwabeland, Stephanie Sheridan, and Cindy Sisler Simms. Every time I saw a work in progress either in person or in an email attachment, I was completely floored by your talents and further inspired to keep writing. You are an amazing group and each one of you added fabulous new ideas to the embellishment part of this book all while making it possible for me to meet my deadline. I absolutely could not have done this without each of you. Thank you!

Table of Contents
Once Upon a Time

Introduction and Inspiration

Several years ago, my quilt guild ran a challenge for its members to create a "puzzle" quilt built around one particular theme of our own choosing. Each month, we were given a block size and/or an element we needed to include in our block that was due that month, and at the end of 8 months or so we had blocks of various sizes all in the same theme which we were to put together however we wanted as long as it ended up square or rectangular. As one might imagine, putting the puzzle together was definitely the hardest part!

My three daughters were 4, 4 and 1 year old at the time I participated in the challenge, and since I spent most of my days not only surrounded by piles of dress up clothes, wands, and shoes, but also catering to the needs of three little girls who were obviously meant to be born into royalty, the theme of "all things princess" was pretty much a no-brainer. My quilting passion seems over the years to have drifted from piecing to machine appliqué, and I had so much fun creating each block and making it fit the criteria we were given. I recall being so proud when I figured out that I could incorporate a heart as per the requirements that month by making it the top of a gown, and the requirement that at least one block be embellished was all the invitation I needed to bead and bauble the heck out of the entire quilt. I attended the challenge reveal meeting sure I would win some sort of award for all my creativity, but not for the first time I severely underestimated the extreme talent in my guild, and "Once Upon a Time" didn't even place. The love my daughters and I had for it was unwavering, however, and it was hung in my youngest daughter's room for many months, until one day I had a fleeting thought that I might be able to share the quilt as a new pattern. More thoughts followed, and eventually more and more ideas flowed into this book, which contains a lot more appliqué shapes and fun embellishment ideas than the original. You'll also be glad to know that the challenges of putting the puzzle together have been ironed out for you already, that is as long as you use one of the layouts illustrated.

As anyone familiar with my design motto of "fun over fuss" knows, I am all about quilting being a joyful expression of creativity, not a precise activity filled with the drudgery of point matching and perfect stitches. These projects reflect my motto perhaps more than any other of my designs to date. They are meant to ignite your creativity while showing that there is no one right way to do anything, and letting loose and just *creating* is what we as quilters should be doing.

I hope you enjoy creating your own one of a kind "Once Upon a Time" quilt for your favorite little princess.

Disclaimer

Going off and creating your own layout from your selection of blocks may cause strife and angst, but as a designer who loves to inspire creativity, I say go for it if you are feeling led in that direction and be sure to send me a photo of your results!

How to Use this Book

Rather than being a project book with a few pages outlining one project and then a few more pages outlining a similarly themed and yet different one entirely, this book is meant to be used as a whole as you create your own one of a kind, never-before-seen, puzzle-style quilt by making choices based on the different blocks, appliqués, layouts, and borders for which directions are given. Kathie Quilter might want to make a long skinny wall hanging using one of the layouts and flex blocks starting on page 26, Barbara Binding might prefer to use a layout for a larger quilt from a layout on page 23 or page 28. Sue Spooler might really like the gown appliqué and want to use it two or three times in different sizes on her quilt, Michelle Pieceful might prefer to make crown appliqués in different colors and forego the gown entirely on her quilt. Angie Template might love the border on page 68, Marie Thimble might prefer the one on page 75. With this setup everyone can be happy, or at least that is the goal, lofty though it may be.

The book is broken into distinct sections – the beginning has good reviews on machine appliqué, embellishment, and other helpful hints, then the actual projects part has directions for Layouts, Background and Filler Blocks, 6" and 12" blocks, Flex Blocks, and Borders. Within each section, you choose what you like and put the resulting choices you make together into your own quilt. Read through all the sections to see what you like and want to include and let your imagination guide you as you prepare to create.

The first section of actual construction directions, after the intros and Getting Started, is dedicated to layouts. This may seem a strange place to start, since most of the time when a quilt project is begun, it is begun with blocks. But the layout is actually the most important decision you will make when creating your princess puzzle quilt; the layout you choose will determine not only the size and shape of the finished quilt, but will show you which blocks and how many of each size you will need to make to make the puzzle fit. It is also where you will get a basic idea of how much fabric you will need (see shaded box for more info).

Be sure to review the sections on machine appliqué and basic embellishment tips before you begin. They'll give you a good overview and will get you thinking about how to do up your blocks even before you start cutting!

But where is the master supply list?

I found out quickly just how lofty the goal of making everyone happy was when it came to trying to determine how to include supply lists for the projects. Because of the design-your-own-quilt nature of this book, combined with not knowing which elements each individual quilter was going to choose for her/his own unique quilt, and all the computations and permutations possible contained within this book, it is virtually impossible for me to create a unique supply list that each quilter can take directly to her quilt shop for her project. So this is where the quilters have to come in and do a little math themselves. (I heard that gasp!) Each layout in the chapter on layouts contains estimates of how much background fabric you will need to complete a quilt top using that layout, and each set of border directions also contains a chart to help you determine how much border fabric you will need. The appliqué shapes can come from lots of fat quarters (you do own some of those, don't you?) or lots of scraps. The more fabrics the merrier when it comes to those appliqués!

Machine Appliqué Overview

There are as many different attitudes about the idea of appliqué as there are quilters, but it does seem to me that we can break the majority of quilters into three categories:

- Those who are avid hand appliquérs and have made at least one Baltimore Album to show off their skills, and though they might not say it out loud, think machine appliqué is a bit of a sell-out,
- Those who love to machine appliqué for the punch layering fabrics on top of one another can give to a project, but who just don't have the time or patience for hand appliqué, and finally,
- Those who run screaming when they hear the word "Appliqué".

I proudly fall into the second category, but don't mind admitting that not so long ago I was squarely in the third category. The point being that even if you think you may still be closer to a screamer than a sewer when it comes to appliqué, you might be more ready than you think to give machine appliqué a try.

Unlike hand appliqué, machine appliqué tends to be quite forgiving, which is one of the main reasons that I, as an imperfectionist quilter by nature, really like it. There is no worry about hiding your stitches; with machine appliqué, the stitches are meant to be seen, and in many cases can become an integral part of the design. When you use the fusible web method that I recommend and will outline in this chapter, there is no need for pins, for turning under edges, or for freaking out about how flat or not so flat your pieces end up on the background. When done well, machine appliqué is just as gorgeous as well done hand appliqué. When done imperfectly, it is still gorgeous and a whole lot of fun. These projects are meant to be nothing but fun, so relax and don't be afraid of the "a" word!

Tips for a Positive, Stress Free, and Fun Machine Appliquéing Experience

- Remember your appliqué shapes are going to appear on the background in the reverse of what you trace. If you prefer a particular shape to look exactly as it appears on the appliqué shapes pages of this book, you will need to reverse it before tracing.

- After tracing the designs onto your fusible web but before fusing them to your appliqué fabrics, trim the fusible shapes about ¼" from the lines you drew, not on the lines themselves. After you fuse the shapes to the outside appliqué fabrics, cut them on the lines. It's just easier that way.

- Don't stifle your creativity when it comes to choosing a thread; matching your thread to your appliqué piece is fine, but using a contrasting or variegated one can give you more stunning results. Of course matching threads hide imperfections more readily than contrasting ones, so your experience and comfort zone will determine which type of thread you ultimately choose.

- Machine appliqué can be done in zig zag, satin, feather, button hole, or even straight stitching depending upon the look you want. Practice different stitches on a scrap piece until you find what you are looking for. Now is the time to play with all those stitches your machine came with that you never use. Even some of the more utilitarian stitches like elastic or stretch stitch can be used as an appliqué stitch if you like the look. To paraphrase Julia Child— You are alone in your sewing room, no one will stop you from doing anything you want to do!

- Appliqué from bottom to top layer. For example, if you are appliquéing the gown, which has four separate pieces, you would do the skirt first, since the bodice overlaps it a bit at the top, then the bodice, and finally each sleeve, since the sleeves sit totally on top of the bodice. The reason for the bottom to top order is so that the places you started and stopped will be covered up by the next layer of appliqué stitching. Cool, right?

- Stitch on top of the appliqué shape very close to the edge, beginning where two shapes come together if applicable (i.e., the place the flower petal touches the flower center). Certain stitches, like zig zag or feather, look best if they are done over the edge of the piece, catching both the piece you are appliquéing and the fabric under it. If you choose satin stitch, it should always be done over the edge of the piece, smoothly fusing the appliqué shape to the background with no raw edges showing through.

To Stabilize or not to Stabilize— a machine appliquér's dilemma.

Most of the time when you see a pattern containing machine appliqué, the supply list will call for a mysterious ingredient called "stabilizer". The very word, when combined with the nerve-wracking idea of actually appliquéing, can be another cause of quilters being afraid to give it a try. After all, we generally don't use stabilizer in piecing, and most quilters probably don't even really know what it is. Let me dispel some of the mystery.

Stabilizer does just what it says – adds an extra layer of stability to the background piece so that as you are appliquéing around the various shapes, your background is less likely to wrinkle or pucker, and your stitches might stay smoother. It can be made of anything, really; some quilters like to use specialty Pellon products designed for the purpose, others recycle old dryer sheets, others use a bit of muslin. All you do to use it is pin it to the back of your appliqué background block before applying your pieces to it. Anything that can be pinned to the back of your appliqué piece will work, but keep in mind that once you are done appliquéing, you will want to be able to tear or cut away the excess stabilizer.

But do you really need it? Opinions on this are as varied as the number of quilters in the world. My own personal opinion is that as long as you are using a pieced background block, stabilizer is generally not going to add any extra stability beyond what your seams on the background already do, so you can probably skip it. The only exception is if you choose to use satin stitch at all, I do recommend using it then as satin stitch does tend to "eat up" the background a little more. But even if you aren't satin stitching, if you feel more comfortable using it, go right ahead. Clear as mud? Great!

Embellishment Overview

Much of the charm and appeal of these princess quilts comes from their embellishments. Whether it is a fanciful jeweled butterfly on the heel of a glass slipper or a floral vine-covered turret on top of a castle, the added embellishments are the stuff that make this quilt more than just another machine appliqué project and truly lend personality to the project.

There is no right or wrong way to embellish a quilt. The past few years have seen a huge surge in beading and crystals added to all sorts of quilts, and quilters are becoming very creative in the ways in which they add that extra spark to their work. Embellishment is a place to let your imagination run wild, and sometimes even to let it get completely out of control. That is the fun of it!

Just about any material can serve some sort of purpose for embellishing a quilt. Let the following list of materials serve as a jumping off point for your imagination. It is only a list of suggested items, and not meant to be a complete list at that, but hopefully it will get you started.

Suggested Embellishment Materials

- Grosgrain and satin ribbons in various widths (anything up to 1" is best)
- Small crystal beads in various colors
- Silk ribbon flowers
- Brightly colored buttons in all sorts of shapes and sizes
- Faceted jewels or beads (the craft store variety, don't go pulling apart your grandmother's emerald bracelet)
- Metallic or solid colored cording
- Lace
- Tulle
- Rick rack in various widths
- Chenille by the inch©
- Braided trims
- Glitter glue—but only if you feel confident in its use! Very easy to ruin your hard work!
- Embroidery floss

If you've never embellished a quilt before, or even if you have, here are some simple tips to make it a fun experience for you:

- A great place to start is with the threads you choose to use when doing your actual machine appliqué; metallic and variegated threads can lend a lot of pop to a simple shape. In addition, a fancy decorative stitch can be not only the method of appliqué, but can start to add a lot of embellishment to the piece as well. Adding details with decorative stitches, like scalloping on a gown hem or shingles on a castle turret, are also fun ways to jazz things up and ease your way into embellishing.

- Move on to some simple beads, buttons, bows, and ribbons either sewn or glued onto the quilt after your quilting is done. Starting simple may lead you to even more ideas as you go.

- Try to think about what would naturally be part of the item you are embellishing. For example, a shoe might have a bow at the toe, a crown might have faceted jewels around the brim, or a flower might have stamens that can be recreated with small beads.

- On the other hand, don't be afraid to step out of the box a bit. No one ever said a castle couldn't have a gold jewel encrusted roof, so if you feel so inclined, encrust it!

- Use found objects wherever you can. Don't we all have a box of buttons that has been passed down for generations? Do we have any idea when we will ever use them, and for what - why not for embellishing a quilt? Or think about that necklace or bracelet that is falling apart and you keep meaning to take it to get it repaired, but it's just costume jewelry so you can't quite justify it. Cut it up already and reincarnate it as quilt bling! I personally have a bag of mardi gras beads that when I can wrestle them away from my children have been cut apart and donated to the embellishment cause on several occasions. Take a look at the "Summer Castle" quilt on page 18... Yes, those are ribbons cut from candy boxes made into flags. The found object possibilities are endless.

- I'm a big fan of being lazy, and I hate hand sewing. So for me fabric glue is the only way to go when embellishing. I love Aleene's Jewel It glue, and there are also plenty of other brands out there that my quilting friends rave about. Since you can glue on about 16 beads in the time it takes to sew on just one, I highly recommend this method, and this particular glue. My quilts travel frequently with and without me and my embellishments stay on without any problem.

- *And perhaps most importantly*, in general, remember that anything you plan to embellish using your sewing machine should be done BEFORE sandwiching and quilting, and anything you plan to add later that is 3D and/or glued on should be done AFTER quilting is complete.

Special Embellishment Techniques

Just a few special techniques that can be accomplished easily with a small amount of effort and make a big impact. Give one, two or all three a try!

How to Make a Rosette
(Photo of shoe—page 20)

To make a rosette, fold your strip of fabric along the long edge and press. Zig zag along all the raw edges to close the strip. Using the longest stitch length on your machine, baste a straight line just above the zig zag stitching.

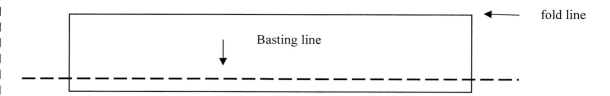

Tie off one end of the basting thread. From the other end, carefully pull the bobbin thread until the strip becomes ruffled up and begins curling back on itself. Roll the strip up following the natural curl it is making to form a large, ruffly yo-yo. Tack with a few stitches on the back to secure.

Gathered Ribbon
(Photo of purple shoe—page 17)

Sometimes a trim is great as is, sometimes it can become even more fabulous with a little extra tweaking. This technique will turn any flat, unwired ribbon into a gorgeously curly 3-dimensional trim in a snap.

To start, measure the area you plan to trim with the gathered ribbon (i.e.- the circumference of a heart, the upper edge of a shoe) and cut a length of ribbon three times longer than the measurement. Example, if the object you are trimming measures 6", you would cut an 18" length of ribbon. Any width of ribbon will work, but it should be noted that the skinnier the ribbon is, the more challenging it can be. I really like the ⅜" width for most applications, but any width can look very cool.

Sew a basting stitch down the middle of the ribbon. Be sure to leave about 4" of thread on either end of the ribbon when you start and when you cut it out of the machine.

Tie off one end of the basting thread. From the other end, carefully start gathering the ribbon by pulling the bobbin thread until the ribbon becomes ruffly and curly. Hand or machine sew the untied end so that it doesn't come ungathered.

Hand stitch the curly strip of ribbon onto your desired object. Isn't that gorgeous?

Outlining Blocks with a Trim
(Cover photo)

This is a really cute and easy way to dress up the whole quilt while you are putting all the blocks together. If you wish to add ribbon, trim, or rick rack to set off the blocks as shown on the cover, you will want to add it immediately after you are done with each seam that will have your chosen trim on it, because once you put more parts of the puzzle together your seam will no longer have raw edges to bury the trim into.

When I added the pink rick rack to the cover quilt, I simply took a long piece of rick rack (basically just unrolled the rick rack from the packaging and left it one large piece), put one end even with the start of the seam I was covering, sewed down the center of the rick rack right through the seam underneath, and snipped it off even with the end of the block when I reached it. Then, when I added another block unit, the end of the rick rack was in the seam allowance and nice and neat.

Creativity Tip:

Covering your seams with a trim not only looks really cute, but it hides any block corners that don't quite meet properly. Take that, Quilt Police!

The Well-Stocked Sewing Room:
Stuff you Just Might Need for this Project

During the writing of this book I came across several items I wanted to recommend that would be good to have on hand for this project, besides the obvious fabric and thread, ruler, cutting mat, and rotary cutter.

A design wall— As you are putting your blocks together, it helps to lay them out on the design wall in the order you have planned for your chosen layout, and a design wall is priceless when you are sewing your blocks together. It doesn't have to be anything fancy: an old sheet or piece of batting tacked up on the wall will work just fine. My own design wall is a piece of foam insulation left over from a home improvement project that I covered with a twin size batting. Pretty clever, and pretty economical if you happen to have just spent a lot of money on a home improvement project, too.

A padded pressing surface—When creating machine appliqué blocks, it can be nice to have a small pressing surface nearby both your sewing machine and cutting area, one that doesn't take up all the floor space of a full sized ironing board. I have friends who have padded a TV table with batting and some old fabric and placed the entire table right next to their sewing machine, but you don't even have to be that fancy if you don't want to. I covered a piece of old board about 24" square with several layers of batting, some old fabric I knew I would never use for quilting, and a staple gun. It sits on the corner of my cutting table along with my iron and is invaluable when I appliqué.

A pressing cloth—Lots of quilters like to use a pressing cloth when fusing their pieces onto their backgrounds for machine appliqué. It's just a cloth you place between your iron and the pieces so that you can leave the iron on the pieces a few seconds longer for better fusing action without risk of burning the pieces. It's also great to use for delicate fabrics, like tulle, which you might choose to use for some of your embellishments. Again, this doesn't have to be fancy; a piece of muslin will suffice, or you can cut apart an old pillowcase like I did. (Raise your hand if by now you are thinking "Wow. This chick is CHEAP! She won't even buy a board or a piece of muslin to use for her supplies.")

A roll of lightweight fusible web– I'm a big fan of Heat N Bond Lite for machine appliqué, and I like to start big projects with a nice fresh roll so that I know I won't run out midway through and stop my momentum. If you have another brand of fusible you like to use, by all means, use it with my blessings. But if you are looking for a new brand, I do suggest Heat N Bond. Whatever fusible you use, *make sure it is the lightweight type*. If you use the wrong stuff (Ultra or "Weight approximation closest to a fireproof tablecloth"), you will not enjoy this or any other machine appliqué project because you will be too busy swearing a blue streak at your thread and needles because they are breaking and bending every 5 stitches. Trust me.

Embellishment glue—If I am simply a big fan of my fusible, I may be the first stalker Aleene's Jewel It glue has experienced. This stuff is incredible. It holds just about any object like you wouldn't believe, dries clear and somewhat flexible, and is even washable. It is honestly like hot glue in a cold form, and without the strings hot glue leaves behind. I use it for all sorts of crafts; a bottle of it is a highly recommended investment.

A fray-stopping product— You might very well end up using some trims and ribbons that will fray if left unchecked at the ends. After all your hard work, you will not want a quilt whose detail elements end in little balls of fuzz, so some sort of fray-stopping product is a nice thing to have. There are wonderful products made especially for this that you can find at your local quilt shop; clear nail polish, which is cheaper and normally something you have on hand anyway, works just as well. Three guesses which one I use.

Some sort of tweezing device - Be it some brand new sewing calipers or the tweezers you have owned since college (but do clean them first if they are normally used for eyebrow plucking), when you are trying to pick up small beads or crystals to add to your quilt, you will find these items invaluable. (Believe it or not, I actually have separate sewing tweezers; it just seemed more sanitary to me, but we all have our different standards here.)

Thread snips—Public Service Announcement: There is a lot of thread in this project. Lots of little seams as you are embellishing, lots of changing thread color in your machine, and LOTS of snipping. Do yourself a favor and use some snips. Wear them on a chain around your neck so as not to lose them.

A light box—I'll be honest. We've learned I am cheap, so my method of tracing anything I need light behind is to tape it to my slider and trace. But admittedly, this does limit my appliquéing to the hours between 7am and 3pm during the winter. A light box was suggested by a tester and I have to agree it might come in handy. She even claims it works great to entertain medium-sized children. Bonus!

Stabilizer—See the call out box on page 7 for my clear and concise thoughts about the use of stabilizer. If you decide to use it, I like the tear away type Pellon makes, and a yard should be plenty for all but the largest of the quilt layouts.

Getting Started on Your Own Masterpiece

Obviously you love every idea contained in this book and cannot wait to get started on your newest UFO. Before you begin, here are some tips on how to break it down as you get going.

- Admire all the photos. I was blessed with some fantastic quilters who came forward in droves to make some samples for me, and I believe every single one of them is stunning— the quilts and quilters alike, of course. Admiring the quilts will not only be like looking at a little quilt show, but it will help you see which appliqué shapes are your favorites and may start you thinking which ones you might like to highlight as larger blocks. It will also allow you to see all the different layouts you might like to try, and start you in the direction of narrowing down that particularly important decision.

- Decide on the layout you would like to use for your quilt. Either make a photocopy of that page (it's okay, I allow photocopies of the *layout diagram pages* – see copyright permissions on the inside front cover for more information) or use a pencil right in the book to map out which appliqués you want to use in your chosen layout and where you want them to go. Of course you are allowed to use a pen, but what if you want to make that layout again using different appliqués? You might be happier with a pencil.

Here is an example of how you might map out your quilt:

	wand	heart
Coach		hat
	castle	tree
necklace	shoe crown	

- Estimate your fabric yardage needs using the information contained in the supply chart for your chosen layout. Since this book is a "create your own project" plan which encourages the use of lots of scraps for the appliqués, exact yardages are nearly impossible for me as the author to give you. But if you use your chosen layout chart from the layout chapter and review what you will need for each individual appliqué block you have chosen, you should find that each quilt will take approximately between **1 ½ to 2 yards total for the background fabrics and 1 to 1 ½ yards total for the appliqués, plus another 1-2 yards for the borders**. But again, use the chart to estimate your fabrics for your particular chosen layout.

- Decide on a color scheme. There are lots of ideas contained in the samples in this book, or you can go off on your own and create a whole new one. (Get used to me telling you to go ahead and try something on your own, I do it a lot in this book!)

- Once you have a color scheme in mind, head to your stash and just start pulling fabrics out that you love which fit that scheme. Don't be shy about grabbing everything you might possibly want to use. Remember: A messy sewing room is a productive sewing room, and you can always put things back later. When choosing your fabrics, try to incorporate whatever fabrics you love, but I suggest you limit the novelty and wild prints to use in appliqué shapes only. The backgrounds work best with subtle prints and tone on tones, or else the appliqués can kind of get lost on them.

- Now is an excellent time to head to the quilt shop to fill in any more colors or more shades of the colors you have chosen if your stash didn't contain every fabric you might possibly need. Besides, what fun is it to start a new project without a new fabric or two? Keep in mind that none of these projects need a ton of any one particular fabric, and 3-5 yards total per project is more than enough.

- Next, check out the section on basic block construction. It will give you several ideas of ways to construct your backgrounds. Choose a few to try; machine appliqué always packs more punch on a pieced background!

- You are ready to start sewing, so let's go!

One More Important Point

Like any predominantly scrappy project, this one can get your workspace pretty messy pretty quickly, especially if you tend to be a creative disaster like myself. We all learned the "clean as you go" method (usually as related to cooking) in high school Home Ec. I would suggest employing it liberally during the creative process so as not to become buried in fabric and trimmings.

Puzzle Quilt Layouts

Each of the different block layouts can be seen made into actual quilts in the color photos on the following pages. If you choose one of these layouts, explicit instructions for how to put the puzzles together step by step are given in this section.

This is not to say that you may not wish to come up with your own layout, using some blank filler blocks of your very own size. Not being one to stifle the creativity of any quilter, I give you my blessing to do any of these things, but if you want a surefire easy layout with all the kinks already worked out, these are for you. One example of the creativity quilters can express with these quilts is already evidenced in the "What Happens at the Palace Stays at the Palace" quilt sample on page 18; the quilter changed up the layout of the 24" x 36" horizontal layout blocks a bit to suit her own tastes. She then had to figure out exactly how to put the puzzle together in the most logical manner, and she did so beautifully.

Each section of this chapter will list the finished measurements of the quilt, both before and after borders, followed by a guide to how many blocks of each size you will need to make to complete it. The estimated fabric amounts for backgrounds, appliqués, backing, and binding are then listed for you in a table format (border fabric amounts will need to be determined using the formulas in the borders chapter); most quilters will choose a layout before proceeding too far with their fairy tale quilt project, so you may find this supply list helpful in determining how much fabric to plan to have on hand. Please keep in mind, however, that these quilts are meant to be scrappy, and you may find that you want to use many more fabrics than are indicated as needed to complete the project. (See "How to Use this Book" section for more details on this). In addition, note that the estimated amounts for the background and appliqués are given in this chapter so that everything will be in one place, but more specifics on how much of those amounts you will need for each background or appliqué are contained in the background block and appliqué chapters. The actual layout map, including finished block measurements follows, after which are step by step instructions on how to put the puzzle together.

> **Construction Tip:**
>
> Pressing the block-joining seams from the back and/or use of a pressing cloth could very well be vital to your level of joy while piecing your quilt top together. After all the work you have put into these blocks already, you don't want to accidentally burn or melt any of the more delicate fabrics or embellishments you may have used.

Photo Gallery

"Enchanted Essentials", 18" x 24" offset wall hanging with piano key border. Pieced and quilted by Barbara Chojnacki.

"*Off to the Ball*", 6" x 24" wall hanging with 2" plain border.. Pieced and quilted by Joany Orsi.

"Ode to Princess Imelda", 12" square with 3" appliquéd bias strip border. Pieced and quilted by Beth Helfter.

"*Winter Castle*" and "*Summer Castle*", 18" x 24" Flex blocks with scrappy rectangle (Winter) and piano key (Summer) borders. Pieced by Jeanne Lex, quilted and embellished by Kathy Schwabeland.

"*What Happens at the Palace Stays at the Palace*", 24" X 36" horizontal layout with unique interpretation of scrappy rectangle border. Pieced, quilted, and embellished by Cindy Sisler Simms.

*"**Once Upon a Time**"* , 24" x 36" vertical layout with scrappy rectangle border. Pieced, quilted and embellished by Deb Donovan.

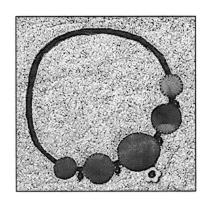

"Fairy Tale Fantasy" , 30" x 24" wall hanging with piano key border. Pieced by Stephanie Sheridan, quilted and embellished by Linda Leathersich.

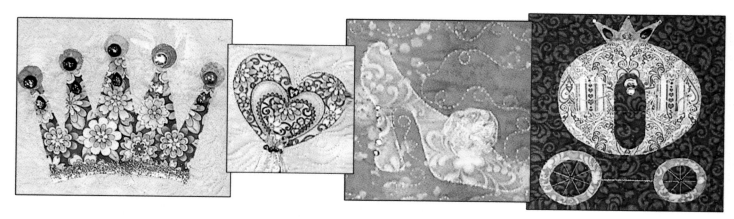

6" x 24" or 12" Square Wall Hangings
(14" x 32" or 20" square after adding borders)

<u>4 blocks</u>

Four 6 ½"

Supply List

Background fabrics	At least 3 fat quarters
Appliqué fabrics	½ yard total using many scraps
Border fabrics	See borders chapter*
Backing	¼ yard
Binding	⅓ yard

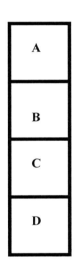

> ### *Creativity Tip:*
> These particular layouts can be fun to do in all the same appliqué motif (e.g.- four crowns or four gowns), but with radically different fabrics and embellishments. (See "Ode to Princess Imelda, page 17)

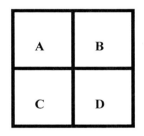

Step by step instructions:
1. Sew block A to the left of block B. Press toward A.
2. Sew block C to the left of block D. Press toward D.
3. Sew A/B unit to the top of C/D unit. Press

This one really is just as simple as it looks.

Step by step instructions:
1. Sew block A to the top of block B.
2. Sew block C to the top of block D.
3. Sew A/B unit to the top of C/D unit.

Special note:

The size of these two layouts are much smaller than the rest in this chapter, therefore a 4" border, which is what each of the border options in the border chapter finish as, may feel a bit overpowering to them. You may wish to cut the border width down to 2" or 3" finished by cutting all of the border pieces 2 ½" or 3 ½" wide rather than 4 ½" wide. Once again, it is just yet another way to customize your quilt to your liking.

30" x 24" Wall Hanging
(38" x 32" after adding borders)

Supply List

Background fabrics	1 ½ yards total (6 fat quarters)
Appliqué fabrics	1 yard total using many scraps
Border fabrics	See borders chapter
Backing	1 yard
Binding	½ yard

```
┌─────────────┬──────────────┬────────┐
│             │   6" x 12"   │  6"    │
│             │      C       │  G     │
│   12"       ├──────────────┼────────┤
│    A        │              │  6"    │
│             │              │  H     │
├─────────────┤    12"       ├────────┤
│             │     D        │  6" x  │
│             │              │  12"   │
│   12"       │              │        │
│    B        ├──────┬───────┤   I    │
│             │  6"  │  6"   │        │
│             │  E   │   F   │        │
└─────────────┴──────┴───────┴────────┘
```

Step by Step Sewing Instructions:

1. Begin with blocks A and B. Sew block A to the top of block B. Press toward block A. Return the unit to the design wall.
1. Sew block E to block F side by side, and press toward block E. Return the unit to the design wall.
2. Sew block C to the top of block D. Press toward block D.
3. Retrieve the E/F unit and sew it to the bottom of block D. Press toward the E/F unit.
4. Sew block G to the top of block H, and press toward block G.
5. Sew block I to the bottom of block H. Press toward block H. Return unit to the design wall.
6. Sew the A/B unit to the C/D/E/F unit. Press to one side.
8. Sew the G/H/I unit to the other side of the C/D/E/F column. Press to one side

24" x 36"/36" x 24" Wall Hanging
(32" x 44"/ 44" x 32" after adding borders)

<u>14 blocks</u>
Two 12 ½"
Eight 6 ½"
Four 6 ½" x 12 ½"

Supply List

Background fabrics	2 yards total (8 fat quarters)
Appliqué fabrics	1 ¼ yard total using many scraps
Border fabrics	See borders chapter
Backing	1 ¼ yard
Binding	⅔ yard

Option 1 Horizontal layout

Step by Step Sewing Instructions (Option 1—horizontal):

1. Sew block A to the top of block B. Press toward A.
2. Sew block C to the bottom of block B. Press toward C.
3. Sew block E to the left side of block F. Press toward block E.
4. Sew E/F unit to the bottom of block D. Press toward D.
5. Sew block G to the bottom of E/F unit. Press toward E/F unit.
6. Sew A/B/C unit to the left side of D/E/F/G unit. Press toward A/B/C.
7. Sew block H to the top of block I. Press toward H.
8. Sew block J to the bottom of block I. Press toward J.
9. Sew H/I/J unit to A/B/C/D/E/F/G unit. Press toward H/I/J.
10. Sew block L to the top of block M. Press toward M.
11. Sew block N to the bottom of block M. Press toward M.
12. Sew L/N/M to the rest of the quilt top. Press toward L/M/N.

Option 2
Vertical layout

6" **A**	**B** 6 x 12""	6" **C**
D 6" **X** 12"	**E** 6" 6" **F**	12" **G**
6" **H** 6" **I**	12" **J**	**K** 6" x 12"
6" **L**	**M** 6" x 12"	6" **N**

Creativity note: This layout has two options since it can be oriented either vertically or horizontally.

Step by Step Sewing Instructions (Option 2—vertical):

1. Sew block A to block B. Press toward block A.
2. Sew block C to other side of block B. Press toward block B. This is the A/B/C unit
3. Sew block E to the top of block F. Press toward block E.
4. Sew block D to the left side of the E/F unit. Press toward E/F unit.
5. Sew block G to the right side of the E/F unit. Press toward G. This is the D/E/F/G unit.
6. Sew A/B/C unit to the top of the D/E/F/G unit. Press toward A/B/C.
7. Sew block H to the top of block I. Press toward block H.
8. Sew H/I unit to the left side of block J. Press toward H/I unit.
9. Sew block K to the right side of block J. Press toward block K. This is the H/I/J/K unit.
10. Sew the H/I/J/K unit to the bottom of the already sewn rows. Press toward H/I/J/K unit.
11. Sew block L to the left side of block M. Press toward block M.
12. Sew block N to the right side of block N. Press toward block M. This is the L/M/N unit.
13. Sew L/M/N unit to the rest of the quilt top. Press toward L/M/N.

18" x 24" Offset Wall Hanging
(26" x 30" after adding borders)

6 blocks
Two 12 ½"
Four 6 ½"
Or Two 6 ½" and One 6 ½" x 12 ½" (see creativity tip)

Supply List

Background fabrics	Minimum of 5 fat quarters
Appliqué fabrics	1 yard total using many scraps
Borders	See borders chapter
Backing	1 yard
Binding	½ yard

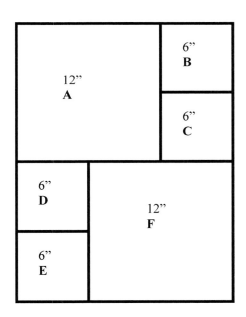

> **Creativity Tip:**
>
> To change the look a bit, replace the B/C or D/E blocks with a single 6" x 12" block.

Step by Step Sewing Instructions:

1. Sew block B to the top of block C. Press toward B.
2. Sew B/C unit to the right side of block A. Press toward A.
3. Sew block D to the top of block E. Press toward E.
4. Sew D/E unit to the left side of block F. Press toward F.
Sew A/B/C unit on top of D/E/F unit. Press toward A/B/C.

18" x 36" Narrow Wall Hanging Using a "Flex Block"
(26" x 42" after adding borders)

Option 1	Option 2
7 blocks	5 blocks
Six 6 ½" One flex block	Three 6 ½" One banner block One flex block

Supply List

Background fabrics	2 ½ yards total (10 fat quarters)
Appliqué fabrics	1 ¾ yards total using many scraps
Border fabrics	See borders chapter
Backing	1 ½ yard
Binding	½ yard

Option 1

6" A	6" B	6" C

18" x 24"
Flex block

18" x 24" block would
be a variation of the
castle or gown

6" D	6" E	6" F

Option 2

6" x 18" banner block

18" x 24"
Flex block

18" x 24" block would
be a variation of the castle or gown

6"	6"	6"

Step by Step Sewing Instructions:

Option 1

1. Sew block A to block B.
2. Sew block C to the A/B unit. Press entire row in one direction.
3. Sew block D to block E.
4. Sew block F to the D/E unit. Press entire row in one direction.

Sew flex block to the bottom of the A/B/C unit. Add the D/E/F unit to the bottom of the flex block. Press both seams toward the flex block.

Option 2

1. Sew banner block to the top of the flex block. Press toward flex block.
2. Sew block A to block B.
3. Sew block C to the A/B unit. Press entire row in one direction.
4. Sew A/B/C unit to the bottom of the flex block. Press toward flex block

48" x 42" Baby Quilt or Large Wall Hanging
(52" x 46" after adding borders)

25 blocks
Nine 12 ½"
Twelve 6 ½"
Four 6 ½" x 12 ½"
(two of each orientation)

Supply List

Background fabrics	3 yards total (12 fat quarters)
Appliqué fabrics	2 yards total using many scraps
Border fabrics	See borders chapter
Backing	2 ¼ yard
Binding	¾ yard

Step by Step Sewing iInstructions:

This layout is big, but if you take it in small sections, it will go together just as easily as the other, smaller layouts. As you are asked to lay a section aside, keep it on your design wall in the area where it will eventually go. This will help you to see how the puzzle is coming together!

1. Sew block B to the left side of block C. Press toward block B.
2. Sew B/C unit to the bottom of block A. Press toward A. Lay unit on your design wall.
3. Sew block D to the top of block E. Press toward block D.
4. Sew D/E unit to the bottom of the A/B/C unit. Press toward A/B/C. Set this unit aside.
5. Sew block F to the left side of block G. Press toward F. Lay unit aside.
6. Sew block P to the top of block Q. Press toward P.
7. Sew F/G unit to the left side of the P/Q unit. Press toward F/G.
8. Sew block U to the right side of the F/G/P/Q unit. Press toward F/G/P/Q. Set this unit aside.
9. Sew block H to the left side of block I. Press toward I.
10. Sew block R to the right side of block I. Press toward R. Set aside.
11. Sew block V to the top of block W. Press toward V.
12. Sew V/W unit to the right side of the H/I/R unit. Press toward V/W.
13. Sew H/I/R/V/W unit to the bottom of the F/G/P/Q/U unit. Press toward H/I/R/V/W unit. Set aside.
14. Sew block L to the left side of block M. Press toward L.
15. Sew block N to the left side of block O. Press toward O.
16. Sew L/M unit to the top of the N/O unit. Press toward N/O.
17. Sew block J to the top of the L/M/N/O unit. Press toward L/M/N/O. Set aside.
18. Sew block K to the left side of block S. Press toward K.
19. Sew block T to the bottom of unit K/S. Press toward K/S.
20. Sew K/S/T unit to the right side of J/L/M/N/O unit. Press toward J/L/M/N/O. Set aside.
21. Sew block X to the top of block Y. Press toward X.
22. Sew X/Y unit to the right of the unit you completed in step 20. Press toward X/Y unit.
23. Sew the unit you completed in step 13 to the unit completed in step 22. Press to the lower unit.
24. Sew the unit you completed in step 4 to the larger unit you just completed. Press seam toward smaller unit.
25. You did it!

Backgrounds for Machine Appliqué Blocks

Before you can start machine appliquéing all of your fun fairy tale shapes, you need something upon which to appliqué them. I really love the look of machine appliqué on a pieced background, but plain blocks can work too. Experiment with using several different background blocks in your quilt and watch it sing!

For each background choice, directions and cutting measurements for the 6 ½" (unfinished) size are given first, then in parenthesis you will find the measurements you will need for the 12 ½" (unfinished) size.

Plain Old 6 ½ (12 ½") Block

Supplies:
6 ½" square (12 ½" square)

What could be simpler? I almost feel like I don't need to give directions, but just to cover all bases, here you go:

1. Choose fabric
2. Cut a 6 ½" (12 ½") square
3. Voila!

Four Patch

Supplies:
Scraps of 4 fabrics measuring at least 4" (7") square each
Or
Scraps of 2 fabrics measuring at least 4" x 8" (7" x 14") each

A	B
B Or C	A or D

I really like the four patch for the background. It's simple, it can be made with small bits of fabric you have left over from other projects, and it really gives a nice weight and stability to the block that helps when you machine appliqué. It can be made with four different fabrics, A, B, C, and D or just two, A and B, as shown.

Step by Step construction:

1. Cut four 3 ½" squares from your chosen background fabrics.
2. Arrange the squares as you would like them to look in the final block.
3. Sew A to B. Press toward A.
4. Sew C (or C) to A (or D). Press toward A (or D).
5. Sew rows together to form the block. Press.

Four Stripes

Supplies:
Scraps of two fabrics measuring at least 5" x 7" (10" x 13") each
Or
Scraps of four fabrics measuring at least 3" x 7" (4" x 13") each

Another simple block that will add some dimension and stability behind your appliqué. Once again, either two fabrics or four work well, for either an ABAB pattern or ABCD pattern. An added bonus is the block can be used two ways, with the seams running vertically or horizontally, so it's like getting two background choices in one.

A
B
A or C
B or D

Step by Step construction:

1. Cut four strips of fabric 2" x 6 ½" (3 ½" x 12 ½").
2. Arrange on your cutting mat or design wall as you would like them to look in the block.
3. Sew A to B, press toward A.
4. Sew A (or C) to B (or D). Press toward A (or C).
5. Sew top two rows to bottom two rows. Press.

Three Stripes (6 ½" only)

Supplies:
Scraps of two fabrics measuring at least 5" x 8" each
Or
Scraps of three fabrics measuring at least 4" x 8" each

This one is slightly less predictable, and again can be used two ways, horizontally or vertically. Use either two fabrics and an ABA pattern, or three with an ABC pattern.

A
B
A or C

Step by step construction:

1. Cut two strips of fabric 2" x 6 ½"
2. Cut one strip of fabric 3 ½" x 6 ½"
3. Sew A to B. Press toward B.
4. Sew A (or C) to B. Press toward B.

Hourglass

Supplies:
Two squares of different fabrics measuring 7 ½" (13 ½") square.

Sure it's made of triangles, but when you construct this block as shown, you won't have any bias edges in the final product. It's a great block to break up some of the horizontal and vertical lines so prevalent in the rest of the backgrounds, and is fantastic because each time you make one block, you actually make two, making the work go faster. And who cares if your points don't match in the middle—you will be appliquéing over it anyway!

Diagram HB 1

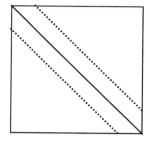

Diagram HB 2

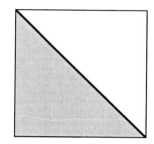

Diagram HB 3

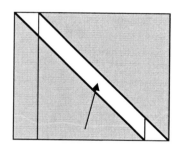

Diagram HB 4

Wrong side of block

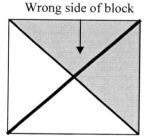

Diagram HB 5

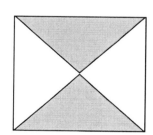

Line up seams so that blocks are aligned on top of one another.

This method makes two of these blocks, so at the end you will have not one, but two background blocks ready for appliqué!

Step by step construction:

1. Place your two 7 ½" (13 ½") squares one on top of the other, right sides together.
2. Draw a line from the upper left corner to the lower right corner, as shown in Diagram HB 1 (solid line).
3. Stitch ¼" from the drawn line on either side as shown in Diagram HB1 (dotted lines).
4. Slice the block in half from corner to corner along solid line. You will now have two blocks made up of half square triangles which look like Diagram HB 2. Press toward the darker fabric. ***NOTE: if your fabrics are pretty much the same value, choose one fabric and press each block toward that same fabric.***
5. Place the two blocks on top of each other with right sides together once again, making sure that the lighter fabric is on top of the darker fabric and the seams are aligned perfectly, as in Diagram HB 3.
6. Draw a line from the lower left corner to the upper right corner, as shown in Diagram HB 4 (heavy solid line).
7. Repeat steps 3 and 4 with this newly drawn line.
8. You should have two blocks that look like Diagram HB 5. Trim them each to 6 ½" (13 ½").

6 ½" x 12 ½" (unfinished) Blocks - Backgrounds

Solid Rectangle

Supplies
  Scrap of fabric measuring 6 ½" x 12 ½" or larger

Okay, so maybe there is a small trick to this one. Instead of cutting your background block out of one fabric using one of your square rulers, you'll cut this one oblong using your regular ruler. But I think you can handle it!

1. Locate fabric.
2. Cut a 6 ½" x 12 ½" rectangle.
3. Voila!

Checkerboard

Supplies:
  Scraps of two fabrics measuring approximately 2 ½" x 22 ½" or equivalent

The following directions assume you will want to make a traditional checkerboard pattern using two fabrics, but if you want a scrappier look, just cut scrap 2 ½" squares and sew them together to in a 3 x 6 grid as shown in Diagram CH 1.

Diagram CH 1

A	B	A	B	A	B
B	A	B	A	B	A
A	B A	A	B	A	B

⟶ Direction of seams

Step by Step instructions:

1. Cut two strips of fabric each measuring 2 ½" x 22 ½". Sew the two strips together along the long edges. Press toward A (note, designate your darker fabric as A to be able to use the diagram arrows).
2. Cut each strip into nine 2 ½" wide A/B units
3. Sew three A/B units together to form a row. Press toward the end with fabric A. Repeat two more times to create three rows.
4. Sew rows together to form the checkerboard block as seen in **Diagram CH1**

Four Stripes

Supplies:
  Scraps of two fabrics measuring approximately 4 ½" x 13" each for ABAB
                              Or
  Scraps of four fabrics measuring approximately 2 ½" x 13" each for ABCD

Diagram 4S 1

A
B
A or C
B or D

Step by Step instructions:

1. Cut four strips of fabric 2" x 12 ½".
2. Arrange on your cutting mat or design wall as you would like them to look in the block.
3. Sew A to B, press toward A.
4. Sew A (or C) to B (or D). Press toward A (or D).
5. Sew top two rows to bottom two rows. Press.

6 ½" x 18 ½" Banner Block

Supplies:

Scraps of four fabrics each measuring at least 2 ½" x 20" for ABCD
   OR
Scraps of two fabrics each measuring at least 4 ½" x 20" for ABAB

Diagram BB 1

A
B
A or C
B or D

Step by Step instructions:

1. Cut four strips 2" x 18 ½"
2. Follow same instructions as for Four Stripes block (above).

Using "Filler" Blocks

Any of the background options may be used as a plain, or filler, block in any layout you have chosen. There is a lot of stuff going on with these quilts, and giving a plain block here and there is a nice way to set off the creativity of the appliqué blocks and help them to stand out a bit more. On some of the layouts that have a lot of blocks, it's also nice to have a few blocks that are done when you are done sewing the background. The "Fairy Tale Fantasy" quilt on page 20 contains several filler blocks that are simply machine quilted and jeweled and are to die for.

Filler blocks are best when they are made in different fabrics from the other background blocks in the quilt, otherwise it might end up looking like you just forgot to finish the block rather than that you meant to do it that way. You may want to use some of the fabrics you are using as your appliqué fabrics to whip up a filler block or two; that way the colors will blend in with the rest of your quilt. Or you might wish to make your filler blocks out of a deeper or lighter tone of the same basic colors you are using for the background (example: if you are using maroons for the background, use light pinks for the filler blocks) to give it some color continuity.

When you are planning your layout, consider using a filler block just to see if you like it. The good news is that even if you end up not liking the look of your quilt with a filler block or two, they are easy enough to change out for another appliqué shape block.

Appliqué Shapes Photo Guide

Coach   Castle   Gown   Princess Hat

Flower   Crown   Word Appliqués

Necklace   Heart   Mirror   Shoe

Gown variation   Kissing tree   Heart variation   Wand

Appliqué Shapes:
Construction and Embellishment
6" and 12" blocks

The appliqué shapes for these two block sizes are shared. You can choose to make any block in this chapter, from the princess cone-shaped hat to the castle, in either a 6" block or a 12" block, depending on which layout you have chosen and which size suits your fancy. The appliqué shapes you will need for the 6" and 12" blocks begin on page 53. Please note that all shapes in the appliqués section of the book are given in the size to be used for the 6" blocks, with the exception of those that are to be used for flex blocks, in which case they are labeled as such and specific directions for their use are included. **If you are using the 6" appliqués for the 12" blocks, you will have to enlarge them 200%.** Depending upon what type of home printer you own, you may be able to do this on your own at home as you go. If your printer does not have enlarging capabilities, any copy center will be happy to do the enlarging for you.

The preceding page shows color photos of each appliqué shape for your reference. Let them both inspire you and be your guide to placement of the individual shapes as you create your appliqué blocks.

Important Words on the Embellishment of these Blocks:

Embellishment ideas and suggested materials for each block are contained in this chapter along with the construction directions. However, there are important things to keep in mind as you plan your embellishment choices.

1. It will behoove you to do a little preplanning of some of your embellishments, because you may want to tuck certain things underneath some of the appliqué elements before they are fused down. Examples of this may be spokes of wheels you might make of ribbon tucked underneath the wheels, or ribbons cascading from a dress or hat.

2. Many of the embellishment ideas are covered in this chapter, but you will want to do much of your embellishment, especially any that involves fabric glue, AFTER you put the blocks together, sandwich and quilt your quilt. Trying to quilt around beads and buttons and bows isn't necessarily a good way to ingratiate yourself to the joys of machine quilting, so please, look over the embellishment ideas as you create your blocks, but save any of the three dimensional additions until *after* your quilting is done. You'll be glad you did.

3. Also, be sure to read the short chapter on "Embellishment" (page 8) for more ideas and tips. Anything you can create can be done, so be sure to bring plenty of imagination.

4. It can be hard to tell when you are done embellishing. It always seems there can be one more addition to make a block or the entire quilt sing. Just remember that you can't do these quilts incorrectly, so embellish your heart out; hopefully you will just know when you are done.

Crown - Construction
Supplies

6"	12"
Completed 6 ½" background block of your choice	Completed 12 ½" background block of your choice
Scrap measuring at least 6" square	Scrap measuring at least 10" square
Approximately 6" square fusible web	Approximately 10" square fusible web

- Locate crown shape on page 54.

- Trace onto paper side of fusible web. This can be done in two ways – either trace the entire crown as a whole, or trace the basic crown and circles at the top separately from one another. I suggest tracing the entire crown as a whole and keeping the shape as one piece **unless** you plan to get creative with fabrics for the circles at the top of the spikes. And if you do plan to get creative, by all means, don't let me stop you! That is what this project is all about.

- Cut out along lines, and fuse the crown to your background fabric. The crown can either be placed with the bottom of the crown parallel to the edge of the bottom of your background block, or tilted diagonally on the block, whichever you prefer.

- Machine appliqué around the edges of the crown to be sure it stays securely on the background.

Crown - Embellishment
Supplies

Both sizes
Faceted "jewels", crystals, trims, buttons

What would a royal crown be without being encrusted with jewels? Place some large faceted beads inside the circles, add a braided metallic trim along the bottom edge, add sparkle with gold, silver, or crystal beads. A little rick rack with some brightly colored buttons as cute "jewels" will create a more casual looking crown, suitable for laundry day at the palace.

Shoe - Construction
Supplies

6"	12"
Completed 6 ½" background block of your choice	Completed 12 ½" background block of your choice
Scrap measuring at least 6" square	Scrap measuring at least 10" square
Approximately 6" square fusible web	Approximately 10" square fusible web

- Locate shoe shape on page 55.

- Trace the shoe onto the paper side of your fusible web.

- Cut out along line, and fuse to your background fabric. The shoe can be fused either parallel to the block edge or slightly tilted, whichever you prefer.

Shoe - Embellishment

Supplies

Both sizes
Sequins, beads, ribbons, etc.
2" x 10" rectangle of fabric if making a rosette (this works for both sizes)

Some shoes are meant to be sensible. These shoes aren't; let whimsy and playfulness overtake practicality for this particular footwear. How about a beaded flower on the heel, or a spangly sequined butterfly on the toe? A 3-dimensional rosette is also fun and can be made from either the same fabric as your shoe or a contrasting one for extra punch (See Special Embellishment Techniques, page 10).

Magic Mirror - Construction

Supplies

6"	12"
Completed 6 ½" background block of your choice	Completed 12 ½" background block of your choice
5" x 5" scrap of tonal fabric, preferably in a light color	9" x 5" scrap of tonal fabric, preferably in a light color
Approximately 6" square fusible web	Approximately 9" square fusible web

- Locate the mirror appliqué shape on page 56.
- Trace one oval mirror onto the paper side of your fusible web. Fuse to the wrong side of your fabric.
- Cut out along line, and fuse the mirror to the background.

Fabric selection tip:

You will probably want to choose a fairly boring fabric for the mirror, something that looks like it could be transparent if viewed in the right light.

Creativity Tip:

To personalize the mirror and delight your princess, use a photo transfer of her face for the fabric.

Magic Mirror - Embellishment

Supplies

Both sizes
Cording or other trim, sequins, flower trims
Threads in coordinating and contrasting colors

Clearly, the magic mirror is the least exciting of any of the appliqué shapes, but on the positive side is the quickest to cut out and get onto the background. But without some embellishment, there is likely to be plenty of question about what the heck that random oval is doing on the quilt, anyway, so let's get to it.

Use a funky decorative or satin stitch in a variegated thread to instantly transform a plain oval into something that looks like it is meant to be framed. Sew metallic cording into curlicues on either side of the mirror, and decorate along the top and sides with sequins, small floral appliqués, or bows. Make it look like a mirror that would undoubtedly say "oh yes, princess, YOU are the fairest in the land!"

Coach – Construction

Supplies

6″	12″
Completed 6 ½″ background block of your choice	Completed 12 ½″ background block of your choice
Scraps of 4 to 5 fabrics measuring at least: • 4″ x 5″ (pumpkin) • 2″ x 5″ (pumpkin) • 3″ x 3″ (wheels) • 2″ x 2″ (stem or crown topper) • 2″ x 4″ (window/door)	Scraps of 4 to 5 fabrics measuring at least: • 7″ x 9″ (pumpkin) • 1″ x 8″ (axel) • 3″ x 5″ (wheels) • 2″ x 4″ (stem or crown topper) • 3″ x 6″ (window/door)
Approximately 8″ square fusible web	Approximately 12″ square fusible web

- Locate coach shapes on page 56.

- Trace 1 stem, 1 large wheel, 1 small wheel and 4 window/door units onto the paper side of your piece of fusible web. Fuse to your selected fabrics and cut out pieces along lines.

- For the pumpkin, you can either trace the entire outside circle once and fuse it to one fabric, or trace each individual section of the pumpkin separately and use several different fabrics to make it a little more interesting and pumpkin-ish. If you choose the former, you can add the lines with some stitching later.

- After removing paper backing, lay your pieces all out on your background before fusing any of them to the background. You want to be able to move things around and be sure it all looks good before you fuse. Lay pieces out using the photo on the page 35 as a guide. The only things that really overlap are the axel over a little bit of the bottom of the pumpkin, and the stem and/or the crown over the top of the pumpkin. Be sure to keep all pieces within ½" of the edge of the block so they don't get cut off in the seam allowances.

- Before fusing the wheels, you may want to add the axel piping (see "coach embellishment" for more information on how to attach it) if you want the axel to appear to be coming out from behind the wheels. Refer to the photo on page 17 ("Enchanted Essentials") for an example that has the axel cording curling up from behind the wheel. It isn't the only way it can be done, but if you choose to do it this way, you will want to sew the axel piping before you fuse the wheels into place.

- Machine appliqué around the outside edges of the pieces to tack everything down. With this block, you can get creative while stitching and add some curved lines to further define the pumpkin and even some spokes on your wheels if you wish.

Coach - Embellishment

Supplies

Both sizes
Sequins, beads, ribbons, buttons, etc. Piping or cording for axel 2 pieces of 2"x 3" Fabric (sheer, tulle, or cotton) for curtains

What would your fantasy ride to the ball look like? Would it sparkle in the moonlight, have filmy curtains in the windows, and silvery spokes on the wheels? Any and all ideas can be employed as you build your ultimate ride.

Use your piping or cording to make a thin axel between the coach and wheels. Refer to the photo of "Enchanted Essentials" on page 17 to see suggested curving shape and placement. Simply zig zag stitch over the cording with a beige or clear thread. Keep the piping longer than you think you will need as you sew it on. Sometimes those loops and curls take up more length than you expect. Snip the end and backstitch or use a fray checking product (I actually prefer clear nail polish over any other product; it's cheap and does the trick nicely.) to prevent the cording from unraveling when you are done with the axel.

To make curtains in the windows, run a basting stitch along one of the 3" ends of your fabric squares, very close to the edge. Gather by pulling the bobbin threads, and sew or glue the top of the curtains to the edges of the window/ door area. Trim to a length you like and tie back using thin ribbons.

Heart - Construction

Supplies

6"	12"
Completed 6 ½" background block of your choice	Completed 12 ½" background block of your choice
Scrap of fabric measuring 5" square (outer heart)	Scrap of fabric 11" square (outer heart)
Scrap of fabric 4" square (inner heart)	Scrap of fabric 9" square (inner heart)
Approximately 9" square fusible web	Approximately 9" square fusible web

- Locate heart appliqués on page 55.

- Trace one each of the inner and outer hearts onto the paper side of your fusible web. Although the hearts are shown one inside the other, make sure when you are tracing that you trace them next to each other on the fusible web, since you will layer one heart on top of the other. Cut out the two hearts along the lines.

- Remove paper backing and fuse hearts to the background. The inner heart can either be placed directly inside the outer or overlapping the edge on one side a bit if you like.

- Machine appliqué around hearts to tack them down.

Heart - Embellishment

Supplies

Both sizes
Sequins, Beads and Ribbons as desired
Threads in coordinating and contrasting colors

The heart is a simple block on its own, so it deserves some serious embellishment. A little rick rack or gathered ribbon sewn on in between the inner and outer hearts can add some fun detail. Colored buttons, sequins, beads, or other small items added either to the hearts themselves or to the background give it some good punch. If you are really creative and have some embroidery stitches on your machine, you might even consider embroidering your princess's name on the heart. Really, anything goes, so go crazy!

Flower- Construction

Supplies

6"	12"
Completed 6 ½" background block of your choice	Completed 12 ½" background block of your choice
Scraps of two or three fabrics measuring at least: 1" x 2" (flower center) 3" x 9" (petals)	Scraps of two or three fabrics measuring at least: 3" x 3" (flower center) 5" x 12" (petals)
Approximately 6" square fusible web	Approximately 9" square fusible web

- Locate flower appliqué shapes on page 53.

- Trace six petals and one center onto the paper side of your fusible web. Fuse the petals to one fabric (or two if you are feeling especially creative) and the center to another fabric. Cut out along the lines.

Fabric selection tips for flower:

This is one of the simpler shapes, so using a wilder fabric will make it pop. Try a pretty paisley or polka dot that fits your overall palette, or alternate one fabric with another for the petals.

- Remove paper backing and arrange your pieces on your background. First place the petals in a circle with the pointed ends of the petals toward the center. The petals should have about ¼" of background showing between them as you place them if you are using the 6 petal set up. Think of it as looking a bit like the mod flowers on your Grandma's (or Mom's, or even your own, I'm not judging) dining room wallpaper from 1961.

- Once your pieces look like a flower shape you can live with, fuse them to the background.
- Machine appliqué around the pieces, petals first and then center, to tack everything down. If your sewing machine has a feather stitch, using it around the petals can give them a nice soft and more natural look.

Creativity Tip #1

You may wish to make your flower look a bit fuller by using more petals. Just trace and cut out as many petals as you think you might like; there are no hard and fast rules that you must use only six!

Creativity Tip #2

Add a flower to one of your "word appliqué" blocks. There is usually plenty of space left over on them, and you can play with reducing or enlarging the appliqué pieces for a size that is complementary to your words.

Flower – Embellishment

Supplies

Both sizes
Sequins, Beads and Ribbons as desired
Threads in coordinating and contrasting colors

Like the heart, the flower block isn't terribly exciting in and of itself, so it needs some good embellishment to dress it up. How about a little swirl of gold or colored trim sewn into the center, or outlining the petals with some sparkling ribbon? Outlining them in chenille lends not only an extra level of color, but also a little softness and tactile interest. As always, beads and baubles of all sorts on both the flower and the background can only up the fancy quotient, and on a flower meant for a princess, there should be plenty of that.

Necklace - Construction

Supplies

6"	12"
Completed 6 ½" background block of your choice	Completed 12 ½" background block of your choice
A total of 10 scraps of several fabrics measuring at least 2" square each *	A total of 13 scraps of several fabrics measuring at least 3 ½" square each *
Approximately 6" square fusible web	Approximately 9" square fusible web

- Locate the necklace appliqué shapes on page 54.

- Trace 9 circles of various sizes for the 6" block, and 12 circles of various sizes for the 12", plus one pendant for either size. * I like to use about 4 different fabrics for the "beads" of the necklace and then another contrasting fabric for the pendant. Fuse to the various fabrics you have chosen. Cut out along the lines.

- Remove paper backing and arrange your pieces on your background, shaping them in an elliptical shape much like a necklace would be if it were draped around a neck. Overlap beads as needed to create the shape you are looking for. Add the pendant at the center bottom of the necklace.

Creativity Tip for Necklace:

If you don't like the shape of the beads given, feel free to reshape them in any way you wish. If you keep them about the same size, though, it will be easiest to fill the block with a circled necklace.

If you prefer a less "pearl necklace"-y look, sew some heavy braid or cording right to the block in the shape you want for your necklace, then add a few fabric beads and/or a pendant.

Necklace – Embellishment

Supplies

Both sizes
Sequins, beads, buttons and cording as desired
Threads in coordinating and contrasting colors

Necklaces are meant to do nothing more than add pizzazz and flair to any outfit, so be sure the necklace you create adds plenty of pizzazz and flair to your quilt. Crystals and sequins will make it shine like a real jewel. Outlining the fabric beads in gold cording or metallic threads can lend a little more shine. Many real life necklaces have smaller "spacer" beads in between the larger ones, so why not add some three dimensional beads between your fabric ones?

Princess Cone Shaped Hat – Construction

Supplies

6"	12"
Completed 6 ½" background block of your choice	Completed 12 ½" background block of your choice
Scrap measuring at least 6" square	Scrap measuring at least 10" square
Approximately 6" square fusible web	Approximately 10" square fusible web

- Locate princess hat shape on page 55.

- Trace 1 hat onto the paper side of your piece of fusible web. Fuse to your selected fabric and cut out along lines.

- Remove paper backing, and fuse the hat to the background. The hat can be arranged so that it is centered and the brim is parallel to the bottom of your background square, or it can be tilted jauntily, whichever you prefer.

Princess Cone Shaped Hat – Embellishment

Supplies

Both sizes
Sequins, beads, buttons as desired
Trims, ribbons, and tulle as desired
Threads in coordinating and contrasting colors

Random question

Has there ever been a more impractical piece of clothing worn by women throughout history than this style of hat? Could it be any more obvious it must have been designed by a man?

The hat is another shape that by itself isn't show stopper, but it is easily dolled up to make it one of the blocks that will get the most attention in your quilt. One of the quickest ways to make it look like an authentic princess hat is to sew some tulle or ribbons to the very point at the top and have them cascade down the side of the hat. You can tack the ribbons or tulle down at the side so that they look like they are flowing with just a few small stitches or some glue. The tulle can also be folded into a triangle and attached at the point for a little different look.

The princess hat in the photo on page 17 features a ribbon chinstrap tied in a bow at the side, because, as tester Deb Donovan put it, "anyone who has ever worn one of these hats knows they don't stay on without a chinstrap." I love the addition and the logic of it.

In addition, any sorts of crystals or bling can be added to the hat to make it sing. Ringing the brim in flowers, or sewing ribbons in a cross hatch pattern, or even appliquéing another smaller decoration onto it are all ideas that can make the hat fit for a princess.

Gown - Construction

Supplies:

6"	12"
Completed 6" background block of your choice	Completed 12" background block of your choice
Scraps of two to four fabrics (see "Fabric Use Tips box") measuring at least 3" x 5" each	Scraps of two or three fabrics measuring at least 7" x 9" each
Approximately 6" square fusible web	Approximately 8" square fusible web

- Locate gown shapes on page 54.

- For the thinner evening gown, trace one skirt, one heart-shaped bodice, and two sleeves onto the paper side of your fusible web. To make the skirt in the fuller style as shown in the sample on the back cover, trace two skirts instead of one.

- Iron all the pieces onto the wrong side of your chosen fabrics, and cut out along the lines.

- **For the thinner gown**, arrange as shown in photo on page 35 onto your block background. Note that the gown fits the block best if it is set on the block diagonally. Place and iron the skirt first, then the heart-shaped bodice, overlapping the two pieces at the waist, and finally add the sleeves at the shoulders. The rounded edge of the sleeves should fit against the top curve of the heart at about a 45 degree angle.

- **For the fuller gown**, cut one of your skirt pieces apart in half the long way, so that you end up with two gown "sides" that look a bit like old fashioned bustles. Arrange your pieces on your block background so that the two halves of the skirt go under the other skirt piece that you did NOT cut in half, as shown on the sample on the back cover, the bodice ends up on top of the skirt so that the point of the heart forms the waist, and the round tops of the sleeves will go on top of the heart.

> *Fabric use tips for gown.*
>
> When I make the gown, I like to use at least two fabrics, one for the skirt and sleeves, and one for the bodice, and I use three fabrics if I am making the skirt with three parts. You can of course use the same fabric for all three dress elements, or combine two or more fabrics any way you choose.

- Machine appliqué around the edges of the pieces in this order – skirt, bodice, sleeves.

Gown – Embellishment

Supplies:

Both sizes
Sequins, Beads and Ribbons as desired
Threads in coordinating and contrasting colors

If you didn't release your inner Vera Wang when selecting fabrics, now is the time to really let her loose. Some of my favorite things to do to decorate the dress are to use a decorative scalloping stitch along the bottom of the skirt and sleeves, iron or glue some crystals all over it in to give subtle sparkle, and tie a thin ribbon and glue it at the waist. Or, while you have your ribbon out, why not lace it down the front of the bodice in a cross hatch pattern and end with a bow at the waist? Sequins or beads could be used to create a shimmering necklace at the neckline. A bit of tulle used as an overskirt and tied back with ribbon is also a fun addition.

Castle – Construction
Pieced and Appliquéd Block

Supplies

6"	12"
Castle Fabric A - 1 strip 1 ¾" x WOF	Castle Fabric A – 1 strip 3" x WOF
Castle Fabric B - 1 strip 1 ¾" x WOF	Castle Fabric B - 1 strip 3" x WOF
Sky Fabric A - 1 strip 1 ¾" x WOF	Sky Fabric A - 1 strip 3" x WOF
Sky Fabric B - 1 strip 1 ¾" x WOF	Sky Fabric B - 1 strip 3" x WOF
Turrets 1 - Scrap of fabric 5" x 5"	Turrets 1 - Scrap of fabric 7" x 7"
Turrets 2 - Scrap of fabric 4" x 4"	Turrets 2 - Scrap of fabric 5" x 5"
Windows/door - Scrap of fabric 3" x 3"	Windows/door - Scrap of fabric 5" x 8"

The castle block is the only one which is pieced, and therefore the only one with cutting directions to make the block itself. The supply list asks for four fabric strips (two for the castle, two for the sky, or background), all with a measurement of 1 ¾" or 3" x WOF. "WOF", or "width of fabric" in this case should be a length of at least 18" but does not need to be a full 44" as is a generally accepted WOF measurement; a strip cut from a fat quarter works great. I like to use two fabrics of similar tone and value for both the castle and the background; e.g.: Two pinks for the castle, two blues for the background. Study the castle block layout diagram on the following page, and refer to it as needed while piecing your block. It isn't a hard block by any means, but you will want to be sure to keep your fabrics straight.

Cutting for 6" block:

Sky Fabric A:
Cut one 1 ¾" x 2 ¼"
Cut one 1 ¾" x 3"
Cut three 1 ¾" squares

Sky Fabric B:
Cut four 1 ¾" squares

Castle Fabric C:
Cut two 1 ¾" x 2 ¾"
Cut one 1 ¾" x 5 ½"

Castle Fabric D:
Cut one 1 ¾" x 4 ¾"
Cut one 1 ¾" x 4 ¼"

Cutting for 12" block:

Sky Fabric A:
Cut one 3" x 5 ½"
Cut one 3" x 4 ½"
Cut three 3" squares

Sky Fabric B:
Cut four 3" squares

Castle Fabric C:
Cut two 3" x 5"
Cut one 3" x 10"

Castle Fabric D:
Cut one 3" x 7 ½"
Cut one 3" x 8 ½"

Castle Block Layout Diagram

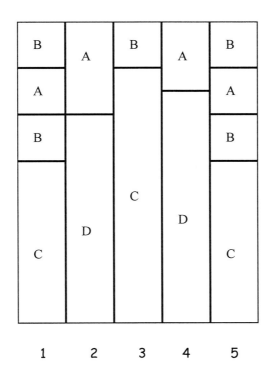

Column numbers   1   2   3   4   5

Step by Step Castle Construction

Refer to Castle layout diagram as needed. Take your time and just take one step at a time.

1. Lay out your cut pieces on your design wall as shown in the castle layout diagram.
2. Sew the pieces of column 1 together, and press toward the sky fabrics.
3. Sew the pieces of column 2 together, and press toward the castle fabric.
4. Sew the pieces of column 3 together, and press toward the sky fabrics.
5. Sew the pieces of column 4 together, and press toward the castle fabrics.
6. Sew the pieces of column 5 together, and press toward the sky fabrics.
7. Press all seams to one side.
8. Trim as needed to make your block 6 ½" or 12 ½" square.
9. Locate appliqué shapes on pages 54 and 56. Trace three triangular turrets, two rectangular turrets, three windows, and one door.
10. Fuse shapes to the wrong sides of your chosen fabrics. Cut out on lines.
11. Fuse triangular turrets to the tops of the three middle towers (columns 2, 3, and 4).
12. Fuse rectangular turrets to the tops of the two outer towers (columns 1 and 5).
13. Fuse windows wherever you like. Fuse door to the bottom middle of column 3.
14. Machine appliqué around all shapes to tack them down. Feel free to use some fun stitches along the way!

6" x 12" and 6" x 18" Banner Blocks

These blocks are good for breaking up all those background squares and giving a little more height and length to your appliqués. All of the layouts in this book use many more squares than rectangles in their designs, so only a few appliqué options are given for this size block. However, as with any part of this book, creativity is always encouraged, and you may wish to adapt a few of the other appliqué shapes into a 6" x 12" or banner size, or come up with something completely new on your own. They are fun shapes to experiment with, so have at it if you wish!

Use the appliqué sizes given for the 6" x 12" blocks, and enlarge them to suit your tastes for the banner block. I personally like between a 141% and 200% enlargement, but you might find that is just a little too big (or small) for your tastes. Feel free to experiment and get exactly

Wand - Construction
Supplies

Completed 6" x 12" background block of your choice

Scraps of three fabrics:
    Wand stem – at least 1" x 8"
    Inner star – at least 3" x 3"
    Outer star – at least 5" x 5"

Approximately 8" x 5" rectangle fusible web (or scraps equivalent to fabric scraps)

- Locate wand shapes on pages 53 and 54. The double star wand is what I prefer to use, but you can also use the heart shape (gown bodice) on page 54 for a little different look.

- Trace all the individual shapes onto the paper side of fusible web. Fuse each piece to the back side of your chosen fabrics.

- Cut out along lines, and fuse the wand to your background block. The stars should be placed one on top of the other, and should overlap the wand stick slightly at one end. Tuck sheer ribbons (see **wand embellishment** below) beneath the stars a bit if you like before fusing.

- Machine appliqué around all edges of the wand and stars to be sure it all stays securely on the background.

Wand- Embellishment
Supplies

Four 5" long pieces of ¾" wide sheer ribbon
Crystals or sequins, glass beads

If your ribbons didn't get tucked under the stars, it isn't too late; just tack them at the base of the stars where they meet the wand stick with a few stitches or even some fabric glue. If you have some larger glass beads, it is fun to string a few on each ribbon and then tie the end of the ribbon with a knot so they don't fall off. Beading a few crystals or sequins in a loopedy-loop pattern around the background can represent the twirling motion a fairy godmother would use when casting her wonderful spells.

Kissing Tree - Construction

Supplies

Completed 6" x 12" background block of your choice

Scraps of at least three fabrics:
    Brown for tree trunk and branches– at least 3" x 8"
    Green for leaves (can use more than one green) – at least 4" x 5"
    Pink for heart

Approximately 8" x 5" rectangle fusible web (or scraps equivalent to fabric scraps)

I wanted to give appliqué shapes for the tree trunk and branches, but in all honesty, they just kept looking way too x-rated for publication. So I am suggesting that it is probably just as easy and looks more natural if you cut the shapes free hand. To do so, simply fuse some blank (i.e.-without any tracings) fusible web to the back of some brown fabric and cut out 6-8 slightly wavy, thin strips for branches and a thicker one about 7" long for a trunk. Leaves can be any shape you like, but I like the pointy oval shape just for ease of freehand cutting and appliquéing.

- After making your freehand trunk and branches, trace one small heart, and approximately 25 leaves (page 53) on to the paper side of your fusible web. Fuse each shape to the back side of your chosen fabrics.

- Cut out along lines and remove the paper backing from all of your shapes.

- Build your tree on your background by laying out all your pieces carefully and arranging them until you are happy with the result. When you are ready to fuse, a pressing cloth is really highly recommended for this appliqué block so that you don't accidentally move your leaves or branches or end up with a leaf or two stuck to your iron.

- Tack down all pieces by machine appliquéing around the edges. Rather than go around each individual leaf, I like to just do some swirly stitching all over the entire leaf area; it's quicker and tends to bring all of the leaves into a unit that looks more like a real tree.

NOTE: using the swirly stitching method suggested for tacking down the leaves is an example of a place where stabilizer might be a good tool to use, since otherwise it may pucker more than you might like. Also, be sure not to make it TOO swirly; simply making sure each leaf is somehow caught with your thread is fine—no need to come close to thread painting with it.

Kissing Tree - Embellishment

Fabric marker
Crystals or sequins, glass beads

What makes this appliqué shape a "kissing tree" for a prince and princess rather than just a plain old tree is the addition of the initials "PC + (fill in your princess's initials here)" to show that Prince Charming has won the heart of yet another beautiful young lady. You can of course use any initials you like. Just write them carefully using a pigma pen on the heart either before or after fusing it to the background. If you have an embroidery machine, you may wish to embroider the initials instead; if that is the case, embroider your fabric before you cut the heart out.

Clear beads glued or sewn onto the leaves give sparkle and look like dewdrops or blossoms..

"Once Upon a Time" or "Princess" Word Appliqués-Construction

Supplies

Completed 6" x 12" background block of your choice
Scraps of fabrics "Once Upon a Time" – one to four fabrics that total about 8" x 8" "Princess" – one fabric approximately 4" x 10"
Approximately 4" x 12" rectangle fusible web (or scraps equivalent to fabric scraps)

• Locate the word appliqués on page 57 or 58. The words will be backward, which is how they need to be to end up on the background in a readable form.

• Trace the words onto the paper side of your fusible web. Fuse the words to the back side of your chosen fabrics.

• Cut out along the lines, and fuse to your background. You can fuse them in a straight line or add a bit of angle to the words if you wish. However you think looks best.

• Tack down with machine appliqué. I like to use a small zig zag stitch as it is the simplest one I know for going around tight corners like you have plenty of with the word appliqués. Be patient as you appliqué the words to the background. The slower you go, the easier it will be, and avoiding unnecessary frustration is always a good idea in quilting.

Word Appliqués - Embellishment

Supplies

Small buttons or flowers
Crystals or sequins, glass beads

You really can never have too much sparkle on these blocks, so jazz it up with plenty of crystal glitz by gluing tiny beads to the letters in a random pattern. Dotting the I's with a small, pretty button or silk flower is a fun touch as well.

Gown Variation - Construction

Completed 6" x 12" background block of your choice

Scraps of two or three fabrics:
    Skirt – at least 5 x 8"
     Bodice – at least 4" x 4"
    Sleeves – at least 6" x 5"

Approximately 10" x 12" rectangle fusible web (or scraps equivalent to fabric scraps)

- Locate gown appliqué shapes on page 54. For this size block, you will need to **enlarge them 150%.**

- Trace one skirt, one heart-shaped bodice, and two sleeves onto the paper side of your fusible web. Because of the narrow nature of this block background, it is not recommended that you make the gown in the fuller style using more skirt pieces. It will be gorgeous as a sleeker dress.

- Iron all the pieces onto the wrong side of your chosen fabrics, and cut out along the lines.

- Arrange the pieces as shown in photo on page 35 onto your block background. Place and iron the skirt first, then the heart-shaped bodice, overlapping the two pieces at the waist, and add the sleeves at the shoulders. The rounded edge of the sleeves should fit against the top curve of the heart at about a 45 degree angle.

Gown Variation – Embellishment

Supplies

Small buttons or flowers
Crystals or sequins, glass beads
Ribbons or trim

As with either the flex block gown or the 6" or 12" gown, your imagination is the best supply to have handy when designing a gown that will turn the head of even the most stoic prince. Starting with some fun stitching during the machine appliqué portion is a great way to start the ideas flowing. Bows at the waist or sleeves, flowers or beads scattered over the skirt, and a necklace of tiny pearls set off with a jeweled pendant are some fun ideas, but don't stop there!

Since the gown shows up in other sizes (6" or 12", flex block) in this book, do check out the embellishment ideas given in those sections as well, especially the call out box on page 66.

Do-it-Yourself Name Appliqué

Supplies

Completed 6" x 12" background block of your choice
Scrap of fabric large enough to fit child's first name
Approximately 4" x 12" rectangle fusible web (or enough to fit child's name).

In the course of the testing and sample making process for this project book, the question arose as to whether or not I would have an alphabet available for use by quilters. As one tester put it "I see this as a project a grandma takes on for her granddaughter, and will want to personalize it." This quilt does lend itself to personalization in so many ways, but since the word appliqués are the absolute hardest to reproduce, and because even if I did provide an alphabet it would only be one font, I chose instead to give guidelines for a do-it-yourself version.

- First, choose a font you like on your computer, or download a whole new one from the internet. I like Script MT, Lucinda Handwriting, and even Edwardian Script if you want something really fancy. Any font will do; it really just depends on the look you are going for. One thing to keep in mind is a cursive type script with all the letters attached to each other is somewhat easier to cut out and appliqué as you don't have a lot of starts and stops.

- Type the name of your chosen princess, using the bolding application, and enlarge the font to as large as you feel you need to in order to fit it on the block so that it looks proportionate. In order to enlarge it more than 72pt, you may need to use another program, such as Adobe Paint. (The "Eva" appliqué in the bottom right corner of the cover quilt was done in Adobe Paint, using Script MT at 250pt.)

- Print out the appliqué onto a sheet of regular copy paper.

- Using a light box or simply by taping the paper up onto a window, trace the name *backwards* onto the paper side of your fusible web. In order to see the name properly to trace it onto the fusible, you may need to first trace it backwards on the back side of the printout you made from the computer and then trace it again onto the fusible. As long as the end result is that the name is backward on the fusible, you are golden.

- Fuse the name to the wrong side of your chosen fabric and cut out along the lines. Fuse to the block and machine appliqué as desired.

Creativity Tip:

Although the directions for the word and name appliqués are all given in this 6" x 12" block section, there is no reason you can't use any of them on a 6" or 12" square block. Shorter names might fit nicely on a 6" block, while "Princess" fits well when it is placed diagonally on a 12" block. It's also fun to add a smaller version of the flower or heart appliqués in the empty space of the word blocks.

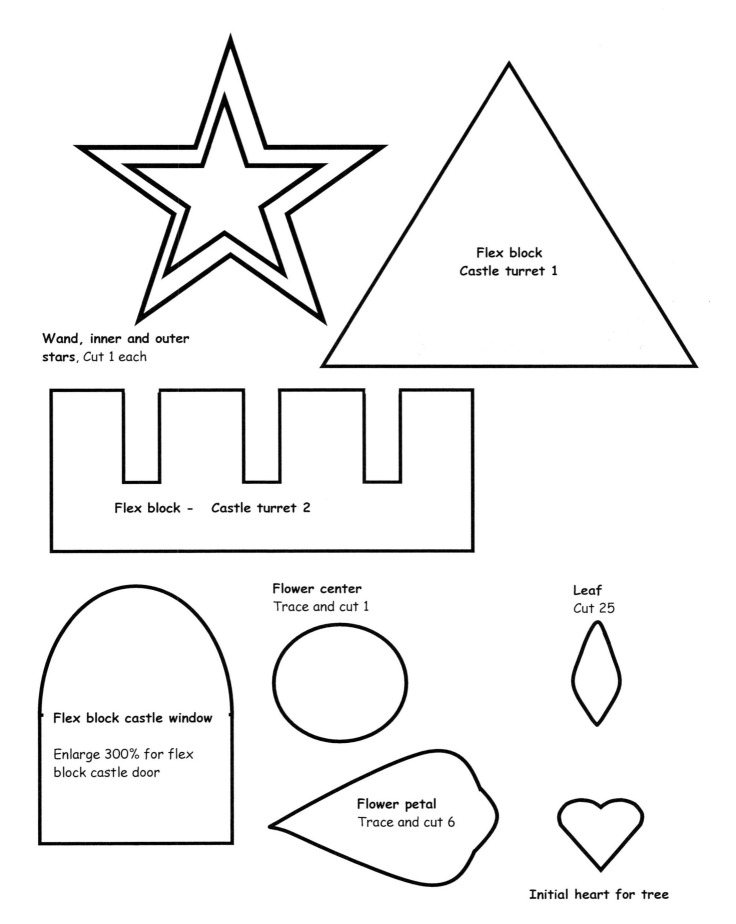

Wand, inner and outer stars, Cut 1 each

Flex block
Castle turret 1

Flex block -   Castle turret 2

Flex block castle window

Enlarge 300% for flex block castle door

Flower center
Trace and cut 1

Leaf
Cut 25

Flower petal
Trace and cut 6

Initial heart for tree

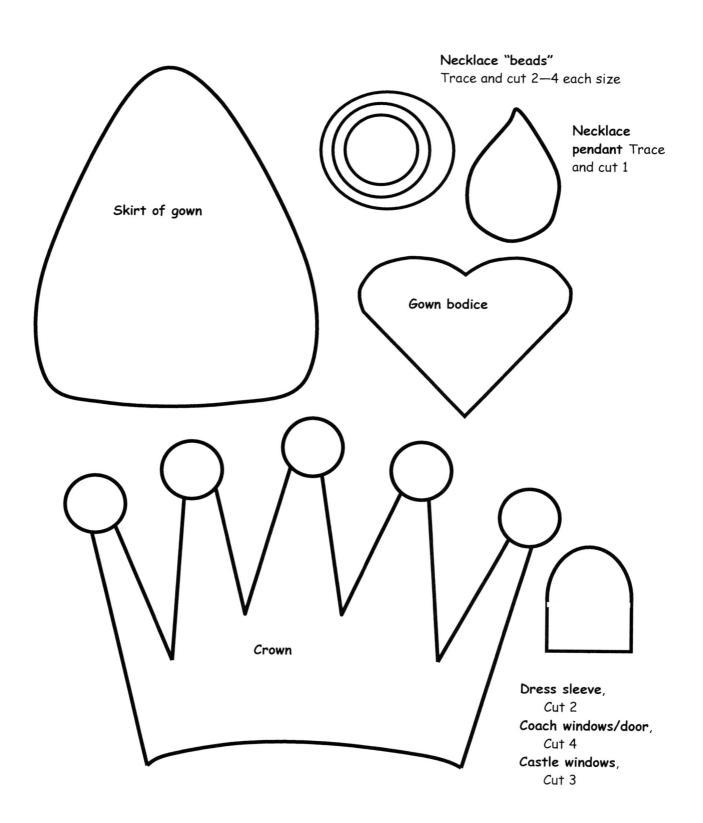

Necklace "beads"
Trace and cut 2—4 each size

Necklace pendant Trace and cut 1

Skirt of gown

Gown bodice

Crown

Dress sleeve,
Cut 2
Coach windows/door,
Cut 4
Castle windows,
Cut 3

Wand stem

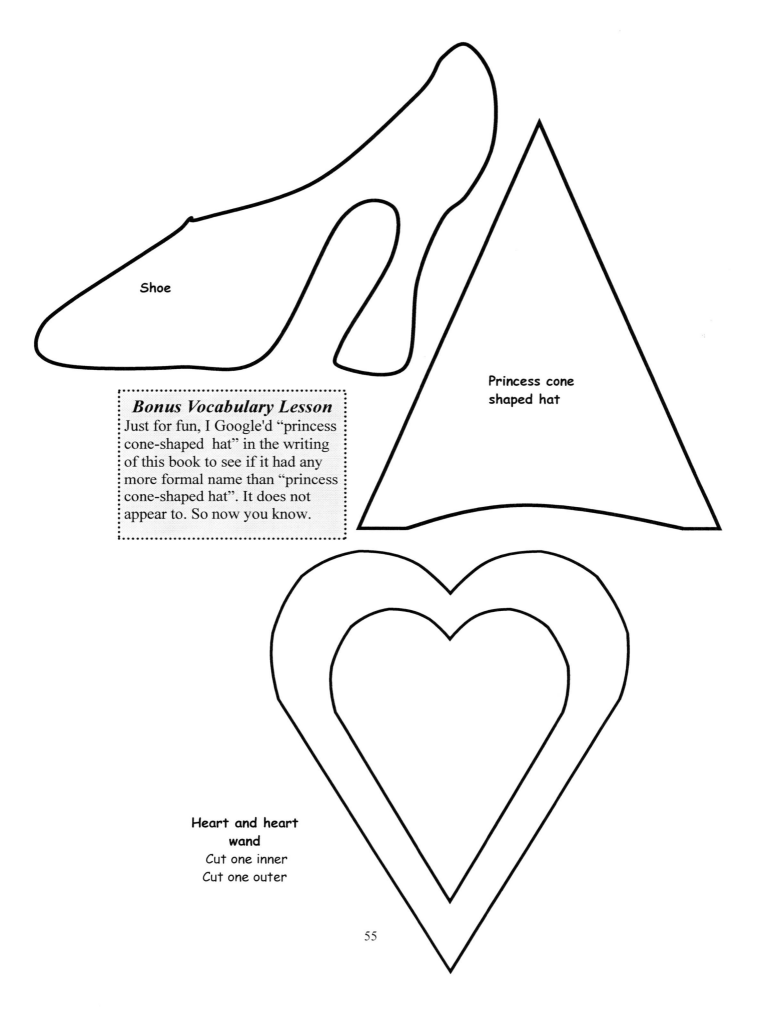

Shoe

Princess cone
shaped hat

Bonus Vocabulary Lesson
Just for fun, I Google'd "princess
cone-shaped hat" in the writing
of this book to see if it had any
more formal name than "princess
cone-shaped hat". It does not
appear to. So now you know.

Heart and heart
wand
Cut one inner
Cut one outer

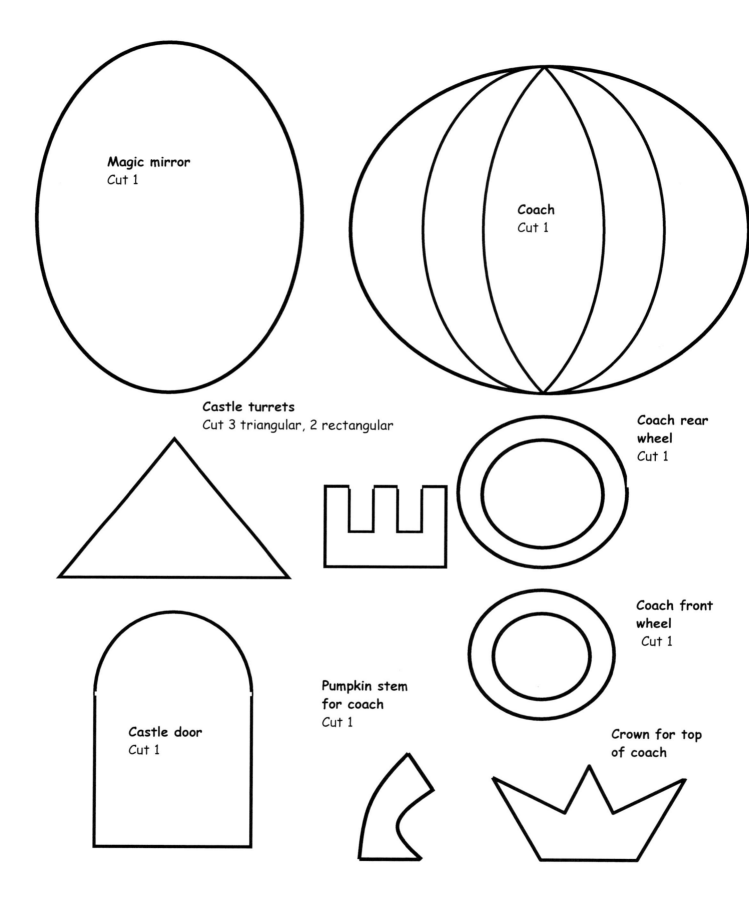

Magic mirror
Cut 1

Coach
Cut 1

Castle turrets
Cut 3 triangular, 2 rectangular

Coach rear wheel
Cut 1

Coach front wheel
Cut 1

Castle door
Cut 1

Pumpkin stem for coach
Cut 1

Crown for top of coach

Upon a Time Appliqués

Use size given for 6" x 12" block

Reduce or enlarge as desired for other sizes

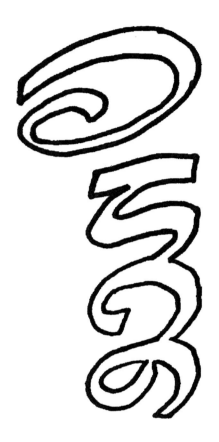

Once and Princess Appliqués
Once – Use size given
Princess – Use as given for 6 x 12
or 12" block or enlarged 150% for
banner block

Flex Blocks
Gown and Castle

I chose to expand upon the designs of these two blocks for no reason other than I liked them the best. While as a mom I am not allowed to love any of one my daughters more than the other (and truly never could, most days anyway), I figure the quilt designer side of me is allowed to play favorites. Since these two blocks are representative of what little girls likely think of first and foremost when they think of Cinderella, and are so much fun to embellish to the hilt, I thought they deserved their own special projects.

Two possible layouts using the flex blocks are given on page 26 in the layouts chapter. But just like the rest of this book, you are welcome to come up with your own.

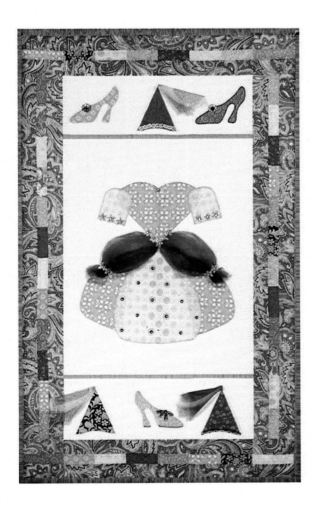

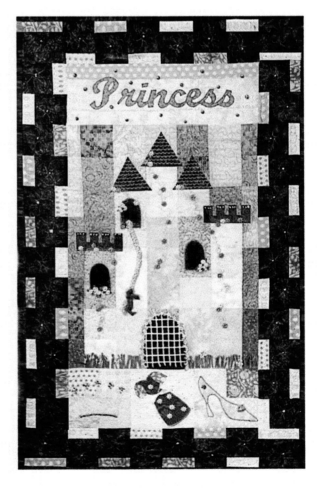

*"**The Princess in the Pea Green**"*. Gown flex block, layout option 1, with scrappy rectangle border. Pieced and quilted by Renae Mathe.

"Rapunzel's Hideaway". Castle flex block, layout option 2 with piano key border. Pieced and quilted by Beth Helfter.

Castle Flex Block

Like the 6" and 12" forms of the castle block, this block is pieced. This time it is an 18" x 24" block, so everything is expanding.

Supplies

The castle flex block can be made either straight two-color, just as the 6" and 12" castle blocks are made, or with a scrappy look. Either way you will use two main fabric colors (one for the castle itself, one for the sky background), but with the scrappy look you will use several different tones and values of each color, rather than just two fabrics in each color. Colors as listed are what I used in my sample quilt, shown on page 59. You are of course free to choose different colors if you like, but the contrast of the castle against the sky is best if only two main colors are used for the block.

	Two color	Scrappy
Castle Fabric A (peach)	¼ yard peach	½ yard total of several peaches
Castle Fabric B (peach)	¼ yard peach in a different tone, print, or value	-
Sky Fabric A (blue/purple)	⅛ yard blue/light purple	¼ yard total of several blue/purples
Sky Fabric B (blue/purple)	⅛ yard blue/light purple in a different tone, print or value	-
Turrets 1 (triangles)	Scraps of dark purple	Scraps of dark purple
Turrets 2 (cut out rectangle)	Scraps of dark pink	Scraps of dark pink
Windows and door	9" square of brown	9" square of brown
Embellishments	Anything you can imagine – see call out box on page for ideas	Anything you can imagine – see call out box on page for ideas

Cutting for Two-Color Flex Block

Castle Fabric A:

- Cut two strips 3 ½" x 18 ½"
- Cut two 3 ½"squares
- Cut one strip 3 ½" x 6 ½"

Castle Fabric B:

- Cut one strip 3 ½" x 21 ½"
- Cut two 3 ½" x 6 ½" strips
- Cut one 3 ½" squares

Sky Fabric C

- Cut one strip 3 ½" x 12 ½"
- Cut one strip 3 ½" x 9 ½"
- Cut two strips 3 ½" x 6 ½"
- Cut one 3 ½" square
- Cut four 1 ½" x 6 ½" strips

Sky Fabric D

- Cut four 1 ½" x 6 ½" strips

Cutting for Scrappy-look Flex Block

Technical Note
If you are going to use a scrappy look, be sure your scraps are at least 3.5" x 6.5" to be usable.

Castle fabrics:
- Cut six 3 ½" squares
- Cut eleven 3 ½" x 6 ½" rectangles

Sky Fabrics:
- Cut six 3 ½" squares
- Cut three 3 ½" x 6 ½" rectangles
- Cut four 1 ½" x 3 ½" rectangles
- Cut six 1 ½" x 6 ½" rectangles

Appliqué Shapes (same for both two color and scrappy)

Note: Appliqué shapes may be prepared while you are cutting the rest of your pieces, or you may wish to wait until after you have constructed the castle block. If you wish to make them before sewing the castle together, be sure to put them in a safe place so you can find them when you are ready to fuse them to the block. Which is by no means meant to imply that your sewing room is as messy as mine.

- Locate Flex block castle shapes on page 53.

- Trace three of Turret 1 and two of Turret 2 to the paper side of your fusible. Fuse to the fabrics you have chosen for those elements. I like to use a darker shade for the triangular turrets and a lighter for the rectangular ones, but it really is just a matter of personal preference. Once the pieces are fused, cut out along the lines.

- Trace three castle windows and one door to the paper side of your fusible. Fuse to your selected fabric. I tend to use the same fabric for all three, but there is absolutely no reason you couldn't use several different ones if you wished. Cut out along the lines.

- Leave the paper backing on the shapes until you are ready to place them on your castle. Set them aside in a safe place. But not so safe that you will never find them again.

Construction

- For a two color quilt, refer to FBTC Diagram on the following page for the layout of your cut pieces. For a scrappy look, lay out your pieces as shown in FBS Diagram found on page 62. Laying out your pieces works best if you are able to have them on some sort of design wall within reach of your sewing machine, but if not, don't despair. Just be sure you can keep the pieces you aren't working with somewhere you can see them while you are sewing the others together; it just makes it easier to keep track of which towers go where.

- Sew your pieces together in columns, and press in the direction of the arrows.

FBTC Diagram	**FBS Diagram**

Two color key

Castle Fabric A

Castle Fabric B

Sky Fabric C

Sky Fabric D

Scrappy fabric key

Solid shapes—
Sky fabrics

Patterned shapes—
Castle fabrics

- Once your columns are sewn together and pressed, you are ready to sew them into the actual block. Again, be sure you can arrange your columns in order on a design wall or other place close to your sewing machine so you don't mess up the order. Add one column at a time, checking to be sure you have the right order of your columns as you go.

- Press all seams in one direction. Your castle block should measure approximately 18 ½" x 24 ½" (unfinished).

- Remove the paper backing from your appliqué shapes, and fuse the turrets to the tops of the columns and the windows and door to the front of the castle as desired. Doesn't that make it look so much more like a real life fairy tale?

- Machine appliqué around all shapes to tack them down. Play with different decorative stitches to give some extra punch to your shapes!

Castle Embellishment

What I love the most about this block is how much fun you can have embellishing it and making it truly a castle fit for a princess; the sky is the limit as far as materials and decorating ideas. Every time I make one I come up with something new to make it fun and adorable. Several of my favorite ideas are listed here; feel free to make up new ones, too!

Embellishment Ideas for Castle Block:

- Colored and decorative (metallic, variegated) threads make great detail elements. Try a bright yellow with a decorative stitch on the turrets, and bright green thread simply meandered around the windows and down the walls to represent ivy or trailing vines. Use a thread in a color that contrasts with your castle wall color to make some lines that will look like bricks.
- *Thin ribbon can be sewn in a criss-cross pattern on the archway door to look like a portcullis. Snip the ends into a point at the bottom and carefully paint with clear nail polish to prevent fraying before sewing them on.*
- Add flowers to the ivy or window box area of the windows either with silk ribbon embroidery, small flowers machine appliquéd, beads, or premade flowers found in the trimmings section of any fabric store.
- *Green ribbons and small flowers make a great garden in front of the castle. Cut 1" – 2" long pieces of ribbon and sew them to the bottom of the block before you add the three complementary blocks.*
- A braid coming from one of the castle windows to represent the Rapunzel story is always a crowd pleaser. Simply braid some embroidery floss and tie it at the end with a bow, then sew or glue it right on to the quilt.
- *Add a three dimensional flag on top of one of the turrets using a prairie point.*
- Let your imagination run wild. If you can dream it, there is probably something in your sewing room that can help you create it!

You'll probably want to do at least some of the embellishment before you add any complimentary blocks to the top or bottom (see "flex blocks layout plan" page 26), and before you sandwich it with backing and batting. A good rule of thumb is to do any embellishment that involves sewing (thread painting, sewing ribbons on, decorative stitches) *before* you sandwich and quilt, and any other types (beading, silk flowers, gluing any items on anywhere) *after* the quilt is sandwiched.

Layouts and Borders

There are two flex block layout options given in the "block layouts" chapter. You may wish to use one of those, or to simply add a border to the flex block itself. Borders can be chosen in the "borders" chapter.

Gown Flex Block

Unlike the castle flex block which is pieced, the gown is really just a larger, more elongated version of the 12" gown block with a few extra pieces to give it a little more pouf. Little girls love to play dress up, and the fancier, sparklier, and flowery the better when it comes to the dress. Release your inner Vera Wang and create a dress fit for a princess!

Supplies

Background fabric A	¼ yard
Background fabric B	¼ yard
Dress bodice *	Scrap of fabric 8" x 8"
Dress sleeves *	Scrap of fabric 8" x 8"
Dress skirt *	Three scraps measuring 10" x 10" each
Fusible web	¼ yard
Embellishments	Threads, ribbons, beads, bows, sequins, tulle….anything you can imagine will likely work to help you create a stunning dress

*Fabric amounts given are for the minimum amount you need for each element of the dress. It is totally up to you whether you use a different fabric for each element, or the same fabric for the bodice and sleeves, or a different fabric for each part of the skirt, or make them all the same fabric. I like to use no more than three fabrics total which all coordinate when I make the gown because I tend to be a little bit too "matchy-matchy" for my own good, but whatever you like and think looks stunning is what you need to use for fabric choices.

Cutting the Background Pieces

There is one portion of the gown flex block which is pieced—the background. Machine appliqué is always easier when the background has some weight to it, and having seams to sew over can actually help avoid needing to use stabilizer. Plus the look of a pieced background with machine appliqué is always just a little more interesting than a plain background. The background for this block is a simple checkerboard using two fabrics, and the cutting is as simple as can be as well.

From Background fabric A:
- Cut six 6 ½" squares

From Background fabric B:
- Cut six 6 ½" squares

Construction of the Background
(Refer to the layout diagram as needed)

Gown background layout

A	B	A	Row 1
B	A	B	Row 2
A	B	A	Row 3
B	A	B	Row 4

- Thinking of your fabrics as A and B, pair up four sets of your squares by placing a B square on top of an A square, *right sides together.*

- Chain stitch all four pairs, snip the threads between the pairs, and press toward the B fabric on each pair.

- Lay the four sewn sets of blocks on your design wall so that they look like the first two columns of the gown background diagram.

- Sew an A square to the end of row 1 and 3, and a B square to the end of rows 2 and 4. Press toward B squares on all rows.

- Sew Row 1 to Row 2, and Row 3 to Row 4. Press seam to either side.

Appliqué Shapes

- Locate the gown appliqué shapes on page 54.

- Enlarge the pieces 200%, then enlarge the resulting copies **another 150%**

- On the paper side of your fusible web, trace two sleeves, one bodice, and three skirts from the larger of the set of enlargements.

- Fuse your shapes to the wrong side of your chosen fabrics, and cut out along the lines.

- Remove the paper backing from your shapes and lay them onto your prepared background piece as shown in the color photo on page 59. You will need to overlap the three parts of the skirt with one entire piece showing on top, overlap the point of the heart bodice into the top center of the skirt, and the sleeves will overlap onto the top of the shoulders of the bodice.

- If you plan to use any sorts of embellishments that you will have to tuck under any of the appliqué pieces, you will need to add them to your gown before you fuse the pieces all to the background. Examples of such embellishments would be ribbons that might cascade down the front of the skirt from the waist, a tulle overskirt tucked under the waistband, or lace tucked under the sleeves at the shoulder "seams". The best way to accomplish adding these is to fuse all the appliqué shapes to the background but keep the place where you will be tucking things under unfused. Once you attach the tulle or ribbon underneath the shape, fuse the entire thing again. BE SURE TO USE A PRESSING CLOTH OR YOU WILL RISK BURNING ANY DELICATE FABRICS.

- Machine appliqué to tack all the pieces down. Remember to begin your appliqué process from the "bottom up", meaning the pieces on the bottom of the stack of appliqué shapes are sewn down first, then you will work your way up to the pieces which are totally on top of other pieces.

Creativity Tip

You are welcome to use this part of the construction process as a segue into embellishment by choosing threads and decorative stitches that will make the different sections of the gown stand out and be fancy.

Gown Embellishment

Here's where you really get to play. Remember this is a fantasy dress, so no idea is too insane to try.

Embellishment Ideas for Gown Flex Block

- Use decorative stitches and variegated thread to machine appliqué all the different shapes down onto the background. Use a different decorative stitch and/or thread for each element. It's amazing how such a simple thing can really start to make the dress look special.

- *Edge the sleeves or bottom of the dress with a lace or ribbon trim.*

- Add piping or sequins to the bodice at the neckline.

- *Tie a thin ribbon bow and attach it to the center waist.*

- Use thin ribbon bows to gather a tulle overskirt

- *Small rosebud ribbons (found in many craft stores) quickly and easily add interest to a skirt or bodice*

- Tiny crystal or silver beads placed strategically over the bodice or skirt add lots of sparkle.

Borders

Is your brain addled by all the decision making in this project yet? The good news is that even though you'll eventually need to decide on how to quilt your project, and you might well have quite a bit of post-quilting embellishing to do and the associated choices that will come up there, at this point you've reached the final construction decision for your princess puzzle quilt – the border choice. Does that make you feel any better? Hope so!

Each of the following borders uses one main fabric for the majority of the border that is meant to set off leftover scraps from the fabrics you used in your appliqués in one of several different ways. The main border fabric might be one of the same fabrics you used in construction of some of your background blocks, or it may be a fabric you haven't yet used but one that just ties the whole thing together. I really find it best to wait to decide what you will use as a main border fabric until the rest of your quilt top is together, because you won't know what look you really want until you can see the quilt as a whole. However, other quilters like to work by starting with the border fabric and building a quilt around it. Either way works.

Because each quilt made using this book will be unique, it isn't possible to give exact yardages for each border without having the quilter do a little bit of measuring and calculating her/himself. The Supply and Cutting Chart for each border style will help you to determine the yardage you will need. A place on the first column under "Yardage" is given so that you may record your length and width measurements for ease of use. Again, I suggest using a pencil when you record; that way, you can erase it easily and reuse it next time you make a border of that type.

> ## More for your Money:
>
> Even if you only use one or two of these borders for the *Once Upon a Time* quilts you will make from this book, I encourage you to use this chapter when you are making all sorts of other quilts. The fabric requirement formulas should work for you whether you are making one of these quilts or making a border for another quilt entirely. For some of the pieced borders, you may need to tweak the block sizes a bit to make them fit, but tweaking should be nothing new to any quilter in my circle.

Scrappy Rectangle Border (SRB)

A simple border that really sets off your leftover scraps. If you don't want it too scrappy, just choose 2-3 fabrics for the scraps and alternate them when you sew them together.

Supply and Cutting Chart

	Main border fabric	Scraps
Yardage formula Length of quilt_____ Width of quilt_____	If length and width measurements are both *less than* 40" – ½ yard If length *OR* width measurement is *more than* 40" – ¾ yard If BOTH length AND width measurements are more than 40" – 1 yard	If length and width measurements are both less than 40" – ¼ yard total If length OR width measurement is more than 40" – ½ yard total If BOTH length AND width measurements are more than 40" – ¾ yard total
Cutting formula	• Cut 4 strips 2" x length of quilt* • Cut 4 strips 2" x width of quilt* • Cut 8 strips 2" x 4.5" (cornerstones) * For quilt tops over 40" on a side, you will need to cut extra strips and piece them together to make them long enough.	• Cut (length of quilt divided by 3 X 2) 3 ½" x 1 ½" rectangles • Cut (width of quilt divided by 3 X 2) 3 ½" x 1 ½" rectangles • Cut four 4 ½" x 1 ½" rectangles (cornerstones)

Border construction

1.   Place all your cut 2" strips of the main border fabric in one area of your sewing space, and the 3 ½" x 1 ½" rectangles nearby.
2.   Construct the side (lengthwise) borders first. Divide the length measurement by 3. The resulting number is equal to the number of scrappy rectangles you will need to sew together in a row for each side border. Example, if your quilt measures 36" long, you will need to choose 12 of your 3 ½" x 1 ½" rectangles to sew together.
3.   Sew the chosen 3 ½" x 1 ½" rectangles together in a long strip at the 1 ½" ends. Press all seams in one direction.
4.   Locate your 2" strips of main fabric which are cut to the same length as your length measurement.
 5. Sew a main fabric strip to either side of the pieced rectangle strip as shown in SRB Diagram 1. Press seams toward pieced strip.

SRB Diagram 1

6.   Repeat for second lengthwise border.
7.   Sew borders to the sides of the quilt. Press toward borders.
8.   Next you will make the top and bottom, or widthwise borders. Divide the widthwise measurement by 3, and sew that number of rectangles together in a long strip as you did for the first two borders. Press all seams in one direction.
9.   Sew a main fabric strip to either side of the pieced rectangle strip as shown in the diagram. Press seams toward pieced strip.
10. Repeat for second widthwise border.
11. Construct cornerstones. Locate the 4 ½" x 2" strips of main fabric you cut, and the 4 ½" x 1 ½" strips of scrap fabrics.
12. Sew a scrap rectangle between two strips of main fabric as shown in SRB Diagram 2. Press toward main fabrics. Repeat to make 4 cornerstones.

SRB Diagram 2

Main fabric

Scrap fabric

Main fabric

13. Sew a cornerstone to either end of the prepared top and bottom border strips. Press toward long border (away from cornerstones)

14. Sew a border to the top and bottom of your quilt. The result should resemble SRB Diagram 3.

SRB Diagram 3

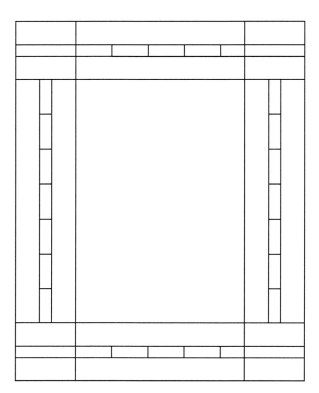

> ***Important Note:***
>
> SRB Diagram 3 is given simply as an example of how this border will basically look. The number of scrappy rectangle units you will use per side may or may not be the same as this diagram depending on the size of your finished top.

"Piano Key" Border (PKB)

This border looks scrappy, but if you use long strips to piece it, it will go together very quickly. If you don't have any long strips of your "scrappy" fabrics available, try cutting 1 ½" x 3 ½" rectangles of scrappy fabrics, and 3 ½" squares of your main border fabric instead.

Supply and Cutting Chart

	Main border fabric	"Scraps" – Use 3-5 fabrics
Yardage formula **Length of quilt**_____ **Width of quilt**_____	If length and width measurements are both *less than* 36" – ½ yard If length *OR* width measurement is *more than 36"* – ¾ yard If BOTH length AND width measurements are more than 36" – **1 yard**	If length and width measurements are both less than 36" – ¼ **yard total** If length OR width measurement is more than 36" – ½ **yard total** If BOTH length AND width measurements are more than 36" – ¾ **yard total**
Cutting formula ***WOF – should equal 40" – 44"**	If length and width measurements are both *less than* 36" – **Cut 4 strips 3 ½" x WOF*** If length *OR* width measurement is *more than 36"* – **Cut 6 strips 3 ½" x WOF** If BOTH length AND width measurements are more than 36" – **Cut 8 strips 1 ½" x WOF**	If length and width measurements are both less than 36" – **Cut 4 strips 1 ½" x WOF** If length OR width measurement is more than 36" – **cut 6 strips 1 ½" x WOF** If BOTH length AND width measurements are more than 36" – **Cut 8 strips 3 ½" x WOF**

Piano Key Border Construction

1. Sew one strip of main fabric to each strip of "scrappy" fabric as shown in PKB Diagram 1. Press toward scrappy fabric.

PKB Diagram 1

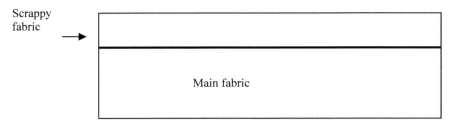

2. Cut one 4 ½" x 4 ½" unit from each strip, then cut the rest of the strip into 3 ½" x 4 ½" units. You should be able to get between 8 and 9 3 ½" x 4 ½" units from each strip. See PKB Diagram 2 for details.

PKB Diagram 2

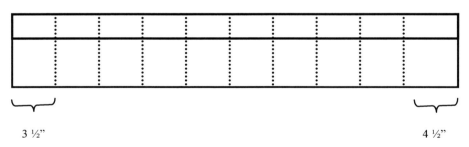

3. Separate your pieces into a 3 ½" x 4 ½" pile and a 4 ½" x 4 ½" pile.
4. Divide your quilt top length measurement by 3. Example, if your quilt top without borders measures 27" long, divide 27 by 3 to equal 9. This is the number of 3 ½" x 4 ½" units you will need to sew together to create each lengthwise border.
5. Lay out the number of border units you will need for one lengthwise border on your design wall as shown in PKB Diagram 3, with the main fabric being the larger part of the unit and the scrappy fabric being the smaller and alternating scrappy fabric up, scrappy fabric down, scrappy fabric up…and so on. Since you have used several different scrappy fabrics to create your border pieces, you should be able to avoid having the same fabrics next to each other very often as you create your borders.

PKB Diagram 3

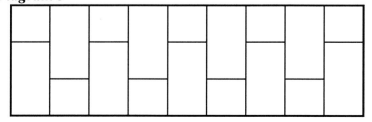

6. Once you have the border the way you like it, sew the units together to create one long border. Press all seams in one direction.
7. Repeat steps 5 and 6 for the second lengthwise border.
8. Sew borders to the lengthwise sides of the quilt., pinning at any seam intersections. Note: You may need to finger press seams on either the quilt top or border to make the seams go in opposite directions before pinning. Press toward borders.
9. Divide the original (before adding side borders) widthwise measurement of your quilt by 3. Example, if before borders were added your quilt was 36" wide, divide 36 by 3 to equal 12. The resulting number is the number of border units you will need for each top and bottom border.
10. Lay out your border units as you did in step 5. When you have them looking as you like them, sew them together into one long strip, and press all seams in one direction.
11. You will need to add the 4 ½" x 4 ½" cornerstones to the either end of the top and bottom units before adding them to the quilt. Depending on how large your quilt top is, you may have several cornerstones to choose from, or just 4 total. Sew one cornerstone to either end of the border strips and press toward the border strip (away from the cornerstones).
12. Sew the borders to the top and bottom of the quilt, pinning at any seam intersections. Press toward borders. The resulting border should resemble PKB Diagram 4.

PKB Diagram 4

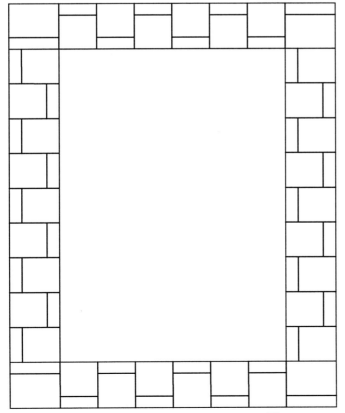

> **Important Note:**
>
> PKB Diagram 4 is given simply as an example of how this border will basically look. The number of scrappy rectangle units you will use per side may or may not be the same as this diagram depending on the size of your top pre-borders.

Plain Border (PB)

Ah, but there is in fact a reason I left the plain border until now, rather than giving it as an option right off. The plain border can be lovely by itself and can set off your quilt top without taking away from the designs you have embellished, or it can be combined with the next border (appliquéd bias strip), so I put them next to each other in the border options. After all the appliqué on the quilt, I thought it best to start the border chapter with some easy piecing instead. I do want you to finish these quilts, after all!

The cutting measurements given are for 4 ½" strips, which will give you a 4" finished border. However, since there is no piecing involved in these borders, it really is entirely up to you if you want a border wider or narrower than 4". Yardage amounts given are sufficient for any borders up to 6 ½" (unfinished); wider borders will have to add more yardage.

Supply and Cutting Chart

	Main Border Fabric
Yardage formula Length of quilt_____ Width of quilt_____	If length and width measurements are both *less than* 40" - ¾ yard If length *OR* width measurement is *more than* 40" - 1 ¼ yard If BOTH length AND width measurements are *more than* 40" - 1 ½ yard
Cutting formula ***WOF – should equal 40" - 44"**	If length and width measurements are both *less than* 40" - Cut 4 strips 4 ½" x WOF* If length *OR* width measurement is *more than* 40' - Cut 6 strips 4 ½" x WOF If BOTH length AND width measurements are *more than* 40" - Cut 8 strips 4 ½" x WOF

1. Cut two borders to the lengthwise measurement of your quilt. For quilts with a lengthwise measurement of more than 40", you may need to sew two border strips together so you can cut them to the proper length.
2. Sew the borders to the sides of your quilt. Press toward borders.
3. Cut two borders to the new quilt top widthwise measurement including the borders you just added. If the new measurement is more than 40". You may need to sew two border strips together so you can cut them to the proper length.
4. Sew the borders to the top and bottom of your quilt. Press toward borders.

Appliquéd Bias Strip Border (ABS)

I love this border; it holds a special place in my heart because it is the border I created for the original challenge quilt that was the inspiration for this entire project. Patience should always be exercised when working with bias, but if you go slowly and take care, it will be well worth it.

Supply and Cutting Chart

	Main Border Fabric	Scrappy Fabric
Yardage formula Length of quilt_____ Width of quilt_____	If length and width measurements are both *less than* 40" – ¾ yard If length *OR* width measurement is *more than* 40" – 1 ¼ yard If BOTH length AND width measurements are more than 40" – 1 ½ yard	Four 12 ½" squares, one each from four fabrics
Cutting formula *WOF – should equal 40" – 44"	If length and width measurements are both *less than* 40" – **Cut 4 strips 4 ½" x WOF*** If length *OR* width measurement is *more than 40'* – **Cut 6 strips 4 ½" x WOF** If BOTH length AND width measurements are *more than* 40" – **Cut 8 strips 4 ½" x WOF**	If length and width measurements are both *less than* 40" – **4 halves of squares** (see step by step directions below) If length *OR* width measurement is *more than 40'* – **6 halves** If BOTH length AND width measurements are *more than* 40" – **8 halves**

Appliquéd Bias Strip Border Construction

1. Follow all directions in the "Plain border" section (page 74) to first add a plain border to your quilt top.
2. To make a continuous binding strip, slice your 12 ½" squares in half diagonally to create two large half square triangles, and pair up two triangles of different fabrics as shown in ABS Diagram 1, right sides together. Stitch along straight edge (dotted line). Press seam open.

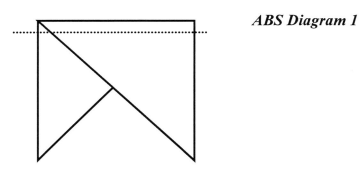

ABS Diagram 1

3. Mark lines on the wrong side of the fabric 1 ½"apart as shown in ABS Diagram 2.

ABS Diagram 2

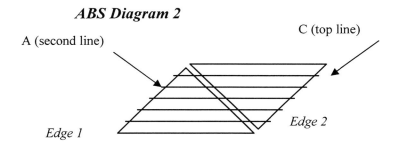

A (second line)

C (top line)

Edge 1

Edge 2

4. Create a tube from your binding by pinning edge 1 to edge 2 right sides together, and offsetting the lines by one so that point A and point C are coming together at one corner, as shown in ABS Diagram 3. Do not line up the lines at A and C exactly, but offset them by about ¼" to allow for the seam allowance. You will have a piece that sort of "sticks up" over the top of the tube since they are offset. Press seam open – this works best by placing the tube over the end of a small ironing

ABS Diagram 3

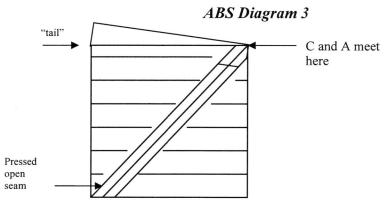

"tail"

C and A meet here

Pressed open seam

5. Using scissors, begin cutting along the line at the top of the tube where there is a tail to start. You should be able to cut the entire piece into one long strip by staying on the line and working your way around and around. If one end is a little narrower than it should be when you are done, just cut it off and discard it.
6. Repeat steps 2 -5 as necessary with the remainder of your half square triangles until you have enough bias strip to go all the way around your quilt top with about 2 feet left over.
7. Sew all your bias strips together into one very long strip.
8. Sew bias strip in half along the long edge, wrong sides together, so that you end up with one very long strip about ¾" wide.
9. Press seam open and so that it is centered at the back of your bias strip as shown in ABS Diagram 4. This can take a little while; I recommend making sure you have something good to watch recorded on your DVR while you do it.

ABS Diagram 4

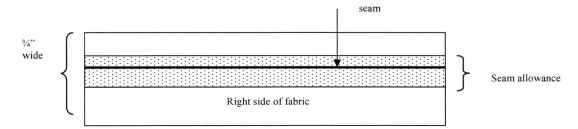

10. Now comes the fun part – sewing it to the middle of your border. Referring to ABS Diagram 5, lay your bias strip on your border so that it gently curves around the quilt center. Pin the border with a moderate amount of pins; don't be too stingy, but do expect that a few curves will move a bit on their own – this is totally fine. Begin and end the bias strip curve at the center bottom of the quilt. DO NOT cut off any excess bias strip you may have after pinning until after you have sewn it on. There is some play in the strip as it is sewn on, and this way you will be ensured that you have enough to meet up at the bottom even if things shift as you are sewing.

11. Beginning at the center bottom where you started to pin the bias strip, sew it onto the quilt using a zig zag or other decorative stitch over one edge of the strip. When you reach the starting point, overlap the end a bit, fold under the top part of the strip to make a smooth edge, stitch it down and cut off the rest of the strip.

12. Sew the other side of the bias strip down in the same manner. Press if desired.

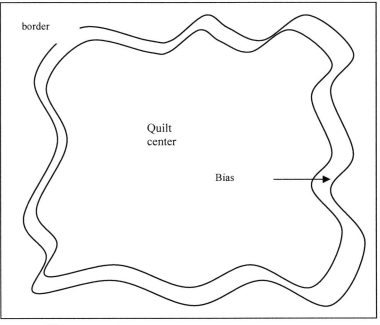

77

Finishing
Quilting Tips

Your fairy tale quilt is complete—well, the top is, anyway! And here is where I am supposed to tell you to sandwich it with batting and backing and throw those dreaded three little words at you :"Quilt As Desired". Instead, I'll give a few suggestions for ways to quilt your princess quilt because I want you to go away from this project thinking good thoughts not only of the project itself, but also of me, so that I might have cause to do my Sally Field impression.

Something to keep in mind as you are preparing to quilt your masterpiece is that you won't be able to do a truly all over pattern because you won't want to quilt over your appliqués, not only because it might be difficult with the bulk, but also because they probably have several embellishments on them already and it just wouldn't work. For this reason, I like quilting each individual block on it's own, because it eliminates a lot of frustration as you might suddenly run into some random embellishment sticking up that you weren't prepared for; when you are basically quilting a pattern around an appliqué, that is less likely to happen. Also, you can individualize the quilting for each block that way, so you aren't stuck with the same pattern everywhere. It only adds more interest.

Suggestion #1—Do I hear an Echo?

You may want to echo quilt about ¼" away from the edges of your appliqués just to tack down the middle part of your blocks a bit. If you use a variegated thread in a color scheme that contrasts to the background, this can be an especially lovely touch. Either continue the echo quilting to fill the block, or use another quilting method to fill in the rest of the background.

Suggestion #2—Stipples, Loops and Swirls, oh my!

They are simple, but they work. Stippling in any size that you are comfortable with sets these quilts off quite nicely; same thing with loops (which by the way can be a lot easier and more natural than stippling, so if you find stippling challenging, try some loops instead) and swirls of any size.

Suggestion #3—Hearts and Flowers on a string

Especially great for borders, expanding the loops or swirls into a chain of daisies or hearts by throwing a flower or heart in every few loops is a simple way to keep a princess theme but add a little excitement to the quilting. There are lots of nice continuous line quilting patterns that would involve these elements out there on the internet, or make up your own.

Suggestion #4—Surprise personalization

If you can sign a name with a pen, it takes only a little more practice to sign it with your machine. Quilt the name of your princess right into the quilt in one place or several; when she finds it someday it will be such a sweet surprise!

Continuous Binding

This is a method of adding a binding that completely changed my life several years ago. Until that time, I had always added bindings in a manner that left a big lump at the place the binding began and ended, but this method makes such a smooth, continuous binding that no one but the most ardent judge should be able to tell where it began or ended. Not that I make a habit of letting ardent judges tell me what I did wrong anyway. I'm including the directions here in the hope of changing a life or two.

1. Miter together 2 ½" strips to make one long strip about 20 inches longer than the circumference of your quilt. Press in half.
2. Beginning at the lower portion of the right side of the quilt and leaving a tail about 10 inches long before you start sewing, sew the binding to the quilt, mitering at the corners and ending about 15 inches shy of where you first started sewing. You will have another long tail at this end.
3. Open the bindings and pull tails together. Fold each back at a 90 degree angle so that the angles are lined up like a miter, as shown in Diagram CB. Press.
4. Pin the two tails along the creases you just pressed into the tails. Sew along the crease.
5. Pull quilt and binding taut to check to be sure your binding is the right length. If it is not, remove seam and try again. Note: the first few times you use this method, you may not get it on the first try, but it does get easier with practice.
6. Cut off tails. Press miter seam open. Press binding closed and sew onto quilt.

Diagram CB

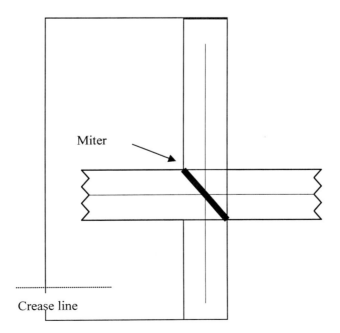

Miter

Crease line

I very much hope you have enjoyed using this book to unleash your creativity and create a one-of-a-kind quilt for one of your favorite princesses. I further hope that you will use many of the ideas, creativity tips, and block and border suggestions in other types of quilts you may design and create in the future. If you have any comments or photos of completed quilts to share (I adore seeing what quilters do with my patterns as a jumping off point!), please contact me and I will happily fawn over your work.

Beth Helfter
EvaPaige Quilt Designs
http://www.evapaigequiltdesigns.com
evapaigequilts@charter.net
www.facebook.com/EvaPaigeQuiltDesigns

Contributors:

Barbara Chojnacki
Six Gables Quilt Designs
www.sixgablesdesigns.com

Deb Donovan
Quilting Enthusiast
dsdonovan23@gmail.com

Stephanie Sheridan and Linda Leathersich
Stitched Together Studios
www.stitchedtogetherstudios.com

Jeanne Lex
Quilt Admirer and Creator
ninepatch@yahoo.com

Renae Mathe
Fabric Obsessor and Quilt Enthusiast
rmtrot@yahoo.com

Joany Orsi
Blank Quilting Fabrics and QuiltWoman.com Designer
www.pickleweed.com

Kathy Schwabeland
spicykathy211@aol.com

Cindy Sisler Simms
Kat Designs
www.cindysimms.net